# What Pe(

"Great book! Thanks for exposing Wall Street and the financial [services] industry for their self-serving, anti-consumer practices. You have created a must-read for [everyone] who is planning for their financial future."

**Kurt H. Jackson, Central Coast Wealth Management, LLC**

"Roccy, I can't believe you (or anyone for that matter) wrote this book. Specifically identifying bad advisors will be a tremendous help to the general public. However, you are going to upset the majority of advisors in our industry. Good for you! This book should have been written years ago."

**John Heyser, Managed Benefits**

"Bold! Gutsy! Powerful! This book exposes industry secrets and is long overdue! Roccy has written an important book for anyone who wants to protect their assets, grow their wealth and secure their financial future."

**Stephen A. Harris, KSP Financial**

"This book was refreshing in that it was hard hitting and direct. This is obviously a great book for consumers, but I would also recommend it as a must-read for anyone in the financial advisory profession."

**Horace Bass, TIG Financial Visions**

"Roccy forthrightly exposes the weaknesses of the entire financial industry. Readers will confirm some suspicions, but more importantly, their eyes will be opened to things they never imagined—good and bad. Chapter 6 especially blew my mind!"

**Lee Martinson, PGA Financial IRA Headquarters**

Bad Advisors:
How to Identify Them & How to Avoid Them

TriArc Advisors, LLC
144 Grand Blvd
Benton Harbor, MI 49022

ISBN-13   978-0-9842308-5-3

Special thanks to Patrick Yore of Brainblaze (www.brainblaze.com) for designing the book cover for Bad Advisors.

# Bad Advisors

## How to Identify Them & How to Avoid Them

**Roccy DeFrancesco**
JD, CWPP™, CAPP™, CMP™

This book is dedicated to everyone who
wonders if their current advisors are giving them the best
advice possible and providing them with advice that is in
their best interest.

I hope you enjoy reading this book as much as I enjoyed writing it.

**Roccy DeFrancesco**
**JD, CWPP™, CAPP™, CMP™**

**Roccy DeFrancesco, JD, CWPP™, CAPP™, CMP™**
is also the author of:

Peace of Mind Planning:
Losing Money is No Longer an Option
www.nolongeranoption.com

Retiring Without Risk
www.retiringwithoutrisk.com

The Home Equity Acceleration Plan (H.E.A.P.™)
www.heaplan.com

The Home Equity Management Guidebook:
How to Achieve Maximum Wealth with Maximum Security

The Doctor's Wealth Preservation Guide

# Table of Contents
# Bad Advisors

## How to Identify Them & How to Avoid Them!

# __Acknowledgements__

With any book that covers financial-planning/wealth-building concepts, it is rare for an author not to have help/input from multiple people or sources. This book is no different.

Always at the top of my list are my two loving children, Lauren and Mitchell. They are my inspiration.

On the technical side of the book, I have several people to thank as this book covers several different subject matters (tax, law, traditional wealth building, cash value life insurance, annuities, fixed indexed annuities, guaranteed return/income products, financial planning, etc.)

In alphabetical order, I'd like to thank the following people for their contributions to this book:

Todd Batson, Marcia DeFrancesco, Roccy DeFrancesco, Sr., Joe Maas, Christopher Mediate, Jon Salomon, Patrick Yore.

# Preface

As you will soon find out, <u>Bad Advisors: How to Identify Them; How to Avoid Them</u> is unlike any book you'll ever read.

As an industry insider (financial, insurance, legal, and accounting industries), I am able to tell you things about each industry that will blow your mind.

The things I can and will tell you will make many advisors cringe when they hear that I've written this book.

The things I can and will tell you will make many advisors worry that their clients will get their hands on this book and will then know the bad advice they've been given.

I do not hold back in this book. You will learn things that non-advisors have no business learning that will be invaluable to you when determining if you are working with "good advisors" or "bad advisors."

Having said that you will learn many secrets of several different industries, this book is limited in length. I considered doing stand-alone books with extreme detail explaining why each type of advisor is a "bad advisor." Taking on such a project would literally take a year, and I didn't want to wait that long to help readers identify several types of "bad advisors."

Believe me, you will receive plenty of details in this book. With the information provided, you'll have no problem determining if you are working with "bad advisors."

However, I wanted to preface this book by making sure that you understand the book is not all-inclusive.

**WHAT IS NOT COVERED IN THIS BOOK?**

In this book, I hammer securities licensed advisors (those who sell stocks, mutual funds, bonds, etc.) for giving bad advice to clients in a non-full disclosure manner and in a way that many times benefits the advisors more so than their clients.

What I don't discuss in any detail is how to determine if your securities licensed advisor is doing the best job possible when picking stocks, mutual funds, bonds, real estate, or other types of investments. I give my opinion of these types of investments and why I don't like them in my book: <u>Peace of Mind Planning: Losing Money is No Longer an Option</u>.

## OTHER AREAS READERS WOULD LIKE COVERED

While I've chosen to write a little over 200 pages in this book vs. 500+ pages that I could have written, that doesn't mean I'm finished giving information to readers about identifying "bad advisors."

I'm constantly writing new articles and I recently came out with my fifth book titled: <u>Peace of Mind Planning: Losing Money is No Longer an Option</u>.

If it is clear that there is an area that I need to cover in this book that I didn't or that I need to expand the information on one or multiple sections of the book, I will do so and will post supplemental information on my website.

If you read this book and find anything unclear or are having problems understanding anything, you can always feel free to e-mail me directly at <u>roccy@badadvisors.com</u> (or if you think you have an emergency situation, you can also call my direct office phone number (269-216-9978)).

# **Foreword**

Bad Advisors is the most important book I've written to date and one I believe will be the most important book most people will ever have the opportunity to read (at least when it comes to financial/retirement planning, tax, and estate-planning concepts).

Why?

The simple and no-nonsense answer is that most Americans receive advice from "bad advisors" where the consequence of the bad advice is often catastrophic.

In this book, I will **pull back the veil** on multiple professions so you can identify "bad advisors" you currently have (and fire them) and ones you will consider using in the future (so you can avoid them).

I am going to give you a **never-before-seen** look inside the legal, accounting, financial, and insurance industries in a way that will **shock and outrage you**.

I am going to tell you what really motivates most of the advisors in each field and how that motivation **taints their advice**.

I will explain to you why many advisors are simply not competent (for multiple reasons such as lack of good training/education or because they are receiving bad or tainted training/education).

This book is dedicated to readers who are trying to determine if they currently have "bad advisors" and how to identify a "good advisor" for future use. I will answer in no uncertain terms the following questions:

1) Is your financial planner a "bad advisor"?

2) Is your life insurance or annuity agent a "bad advisor"?

3) Is your attorney a "bad advisor"?

4) Is your CPA/EA/accountant a "bad advisor"?

5) What are the consequences of using a "bad advisor"?

And, finally, (and just as important as identifying a "bad advisor"):

6) How do you identify and find a "good advisor"?

## WHAT IS A "GOOD ADVISOR"?

I wrote this book not just so you could identify "bad advisors" but also so you could identify "good advisors." A "good advisor" has the following characteristics:

### 1) Professionally competent.

As you'll find out, many advisors are not professionally competent (in layman's terms they really don't know what they are doing, you just don't know it). A competent advisor will keep up with the trends in his/her industry (laws and/or the tax code if an attorney/CPA or financial/insurance products or tools if a financial planner or insurance agent). Advisors who do not keep up with the times will quickly become less competent and, ultimately, incompetent over time.

I can't count the number of times I've received calls from advisors who've told me they have been in the business for 20-30 years (insurance/financial business) and are calling me for information on the most basic issues or to learn about products they didn't know about that are viable and have been in existence for over ten years.

### 2) The ability to make recommendations.

Too often advisors lay out options for clients and let the clients choose what to do. People hire or use professionals because they are supposed to know what they are doing (more so than the clients) and so they can recommend what they believe is best.

Advisors refrain from making recommendations many times because they are afraid of being wrong and do not want to take full responsibility for their recommendations. Competent advisors will make specific recommendations and help their clients implement a course of action after it has been chosen.

**3) The ability to know when help is needed and if the advisor is over his/her head.**

A good advisor will not act like they know what they are doing when they don't just to make a sale. Unfortunately, this happens all the time because the client does not understand the subject matter or product being discussed and because the salesperson is good at selling himself/herself as a credible/competent advisor.

A "good advisor" will have a team of professionals or a support network (like The Wealth Preservation Institute) to lean on to help clients so the best advice can ultimately be given.

**4) Always providing advice that is in the client's best interest not the advisor's best interest.**

This is really the big one (especially in the insurance and financial-services fields). What you will read in this book will absolutely frighten you. It will also enrage you when you find out that many advisors have no intention of doing what's in their client's best interest. In fact, you will learn how many advisors are forbidden from providing clients the best advice by their employers or firms where their licenses are held.

Being a "good advisor" is simple—all you have to do is know what you are doing and give advice that is in the client's best interest.

If it's so simple then it would make sense that most advisors are "good advisors," right? I'll let you make the determination for yourself after you read this book, but it is my informed opinion that a significant portion of advisors are not "good advisors" but are, in fact, "bad advisors."

If you would like to find a "good advisor" in your local area to work with or simply to review advice given to you by what you think is a "bad advisor," go to www.badadvisors.com where you can request information on the advisors in your area.

### WHO AM I TO DETERMINE WHO IS A "GOOD" AND "BAD ADVISOR"?

My name is **Roccy DeFrancesco, Jr., JD, CWPP™, CAPP™, CMP™**, and it is my job to educate CPAs/EAs/accountants, attorneys, financial planners, and life insurance agents on how to provide the "best" advice to their clients.

Let me answer the question that you may have when you read the above paragraph of what I do for a living. Yes, I'm an educator; but before moving into the education space, I practiced law for a period of years after which I provided financial planning and insurance/annuity advice to clients all over the country.

My point is that I want to dispel any notion that you may have that I am just some pundit who hasn't been in the real world giving advice to clients. I've been there, done that, and found a higher calling for myself which I fulfill through my company, The Wealth Preservation Institute.

In all of my books, I put in a bio section because I think it's important for readers to know about the author's background (so readers can determine by my background if there's a good likelihood that I know what I'm talking about).

Because this book will challenge your perception of every advisor you've ever had and every advisor you will ever have, it is more important than ever for you to learn about my background.

So, if you'll indulge me, I will lay out my background and why I am uniquely qualified to write a book with such a bold title as <u>Bad Advisors: How to Identify Them; How to Avoid Them</u>.

Let me start with a discussion about my background by going back to my last year of undergraduate studies at Embry Riddle Aeronautical University in 1992. In 1992, I was a commercial pilot looking to graduate undergrad in 1993 and start looking for a job. As it turned out, the airline industry was in a tailspin (pun intended); and you could not find a job anywhere (and, if you found one, it was a very low-paying job). Actually, to get a job, you had to pay the airlines for your own training (which usually exceeded $10,000).

Thinking that flying would be a fun career, but not the only possible one, I contacted my parents and asked them what they would think if I decided not to work as a pilot and instead go to law school.

To my surprise, they were very supportive of the move; and so in 1993, I started law school at Valparaiso University School of Law.

While in law school, I decided that I wanted to be a personal injury attorney (you see them typically on the back of your phone books). I had family friends who did that type of law, and they seemed happy and made more money than other attorneys in my home town. Therefore, when taking elective courses in law school, I concentrated on personal injury courses.

When I graduated from law school (similar to the airline industry), personal injury law was on the downswing due to "tort reform." Therefore, few firms were hiring in the area where I wanted to live.

As it turned out, I could not find a job that I wanted; and so in 1996, I ended up coming back to my home town of St. Joseph, Michigan, to practice law with my father, Roccy M. DeFrancesco, Sr., JD. My areas of practice were business law (setting up corporations), real estate law, a little personal injury law, and a heavy emphasis on estate planning and divorce law.

I was truly amazed at how much Roccy, Sr., knew and was more than happy to make virtually no money while learning as much as I could from him.

As it turns out, I've got one of those personalities where I'm always searching for that next challenge in life. The next challenge was to still become a personal injury attorney. After a year or so of working with Roccy, Sr., I found out that our local personal injury firm in town was hiring (a rare occasion). The firm was founded by a long-time family friend who after an interview process hired me to be their new associate in the summer of 1997.

During that summer, I blew out my knee playing with my dog in the yard and had it operated on by another long-time family friend, Dr. Sterling Doster, and his new sports-fellowship-trained surgeon, Dr. Gregory Fox. Most people stop me when I'm going through the twisted story of why I do what I do for a living and ask why I tell people I blew my knee out. The answer is simple—blowing my knee out and having it operated on ended up being a life-altering event as you will see.

On one of the follow-up visits with the doctors who fixed my knee (their office was in Bloomington, Indiana, which was four hours south of where I lived at the time), we all went out to dinner. After a few glasses of wine, the doctors asked me if I wanted to come down to Bloomington to run their medical practice. They said their office manager was getting in over her head and that they'd double my salary to come run their practice.

I told them I could not possibly entertain accepting their offer since I just took a new job with the local personal injury law firm in town. After dinner, I went home and continued to work at the law firm. As it turned out and through no fault of the new employer, I really didn't enjoy the personal injury work I was doing.

Therefore, after working at the new firm for a few months, I called the doctors back and asked them if they were serious about me running their medical practice. They said they had a few glasses of wine that night and sort of remembered the conversation. They asked for a few days to talk about it and a week later called me and told me to come down to Bloomington, Indiana, to run their medical clinic.

When I told the attorneys who hired me at the personal injury firm that the medical practice was going to double my salary, they laughed a bit and wished me well. I didn't expect them to match that offer; and as I said, they were long-time family friends, and they simply wanted the best for me.

When I moved down to Bloomington, Indiana, in January of 1998, my wife was pregnant with our first child and things were moving quickly. The lady who was supposed to train me took six weeks of sick time and then quit. I learned on the fly how to run the medical practice, which took a good six months.

As it turned out, I was a <u>terrible manager of people; but I was a whiz with the finances</u>. Understand that I came out of a litigation practice where I went to war every day with other attorneys on behalf of my clients (especially the divorces I used to work on). Then suddenly I ended up running a medical clinic with thirteen female employees who worked under an office manager who really did not give much direction.

Needless to say, I did a very poor job of managing the staff the first six months. The finances of the office, on the other hand, were another matter. Since I had no faith in the previous office manager, I decided to shop every vendor the medical practice used to see if I could save the office some money.

As it turned out, I saved the four-physician medical office over $35,000 in expenses my first year. On what? Health insurance, malpractice insurance, office supply purchasing, outside professional help, collections expenses, and overtime; and I successfully helped negotiate a very difficult purchase of the medical office building the practice rented.

After about six months, I had things in the office the way I wanted them from a financial point of view. While I did not always get along with the staff, I have to give them their due in that most of them were top notch and did a tremendous job in their particular specialty. What that left me with, however, was a dilemma.

After fixing the office financially and because the staff did not require much oversight from me, I had a tremendous amount of free time on my hands. I could run the medical office for what I needed to do as a manager in two-to-four hours or less each day. Remember, that in the practice of law, I used to have 25+ clients all wanting something from me; and now I was running a medical office with fewer than 20 employees. If I didn't come to work for weeks on end, the office would run just fine.

The physicians at the medical office knew I would get to the point of being bored and thought I would open up a small legal practice out of the medical office or that I would play golf every day. **Instead of doing either, I decided to research in extraordinary detail "advanced" planning for high-income/net-worth clients** (who were my physician employers).

People wonder how I was able to create three advanced education/certification courses with over 1,300 pages of text and two books by the age of 37. It's really not that I'm any brighter than anyone else or anyone reading this book. It's that, due to the extraordinary circumstances of my employment at the medical practice, I was able to spend two-and-a-half years researching: asset protection, income, estate and capital gains tax planning/reduction, corporate structure, advanced estate planning, long-term care, disability and life insurance, annuities, mortgages, and the list goes on and on.

After my research on a topic, I would write an article on it and get it published in any number of places including, but not limited to, the following: Orthopedics Today, Physician Money Digest, Physician's News Digest, MomMD, American Urological Association Newsletter, Today in Cardiology, The Rake Report by Price Waterhouse Coopers, The CPA Journal, CPA Wealth Provider, Strategic Orthopaedics, General Surgery News, the Indiana Bar Journal, the OH CPA Newsletter, Financial Planning Magazine, and Insurance Selling Magazine.

Then I started doing educational seminars for the following organizations (not an exhaustive list): Indiana State Medical Association, Ohio State Medical Association, Academy of Medicine of Cincinnati, Mid-America Orthopaedic Association, the MI, OH, IN, and KY CPA Societies, Professional Association of Health Care Office Management (PAHCOM), BONES, the American Academy of Medical Management, TX Medical Group Management Association (TX MGMA), Texas Medical Association Insurance Trust (TMAIT), the Michigan Orthodontics Association, the National Funeral Home Directors Association, the Society of Financial Service Professionals, the National Association of Insurance and Financial Advisors, and more.

After awhile, you have enough content from articles and speaking engagements to write a book; so I wrote my first book, The Doctor's Wealth Preservation Guide.

## MOVING ON FROM THE MEDICAL PRACTICE

While at the medical practice, I started two separate consulting companies—one company where I would provide advice to physicians and one company to work with advisors who wanted help with their physicians and other clients.

As it turned out, I made enough money from the side consulting businesses to allow myself to try consulting full time. By then my wife was pregnant with our second child; and since the family didn't visit us much in Bloomington, Indiana, we also wanted to move back to Michigan so we could be closer to them.

That's just what we did in the spring of 2000. My wife, daughter, and soon-to-be son moved back to my home town of St. Joseph, Michigan, where I worked with my two companies to help physicians with asset protection, estate and tax planning, and advisors who had physicians or other high-income/net-worth clients who needed help.

The good news is that I was making a good living with my two consulting companies. The bad news is that after a while I became miserable. I don't want to sound like I was crying with a loaf of bread under my arm; but I was traveling a lot to visit clients and advisors around the country as well as doing several seminars, and I was getting worn out. It's not that I didn't enjoy it; but with two young children, I was looking for a business model that would let me go to their ball games, go to the pool, and work in the yard (although I despise yard work).

## THE LIGHT BULB GOES ON

I was in Las Vegas in 2004 giving a seminar for the National Society of Accountants (NSA) when the light bulb finally went on for me. A friend of mine (who introduced me to the NSA) and I were out to dinner in between the days of the seminar, and I was complaining to him about how I was making decent money but that I was really getting worn out. I basically had made the decision that I needed to do something else, and I was even considering going back to practicing law (it's hard to even type that and see it in print).

My friend told me to stop complaining and then off the cuff said: "Roccy, what you need to do is create your own Roccy-certification course. You need the School of Roccy."

Of course, he was making fun of me, which I'm sure I deserved, but he was onto something and didn't know it. He had heard me speak many times and read my book, The Doctor's Wealth Preservation Guide. As someone "in the industry," he knew that the topics I dealt with in my book and spoke about at seminars were fairly unique and that other advisors who have or want to have high-income/net-worth clients would like to learn these topics.

Like the day I decided to take the job running the medical practice, that day in Vegas was again one of those days in your life you look back on and see it as life altering.

I went home from the Vegas NSA seminar and thought about putting my own educational program together. I figured I could put the program together with no problem. I had a lot of content and some of the best experts in the country who were nice enough to let me bend their ear on advanced-planning topics. The question was: Could I make a living doing "education?"

I said to myself that it really didn't matter since I didn't want to continue traveling no matter how much money could be made. Therefore, I told my wife that I was changing course, and I hoped for everyone's sake it would work out. I decided to put together what I now call the only "advanced" education/certification courses in the country where I educate CPAs/EAs/accountants, attorneys, financial planners, mortgage brokers, security traders, etc., on advanced planning for high-income/net-worth clients.

I formed my own educational institute with an educational board of some of the country's best experts in their fields.

The courses are the Certified Wealth Preservation Planner (CWPP™), Certified Asset Protection Planner, (CAPP™), and Certified Medicaid Planner (CMP™). Each course requires advisors to read over hundreds of pages of text, take a lengthy multiple-choice/true-false test, and pass an essay test. The essay test confirms to me that the advisors who take the courses not only understand the material but can apply it in the "real world."

I rolled the CWPP™ and CAPP™ courses out in 2005 and have had a nice steady flow of advisors sign up to take the courses online or in person. In 2010, I rolled out the CMP™ course.

I'm proud to say that the reviews from those who have taken the courses have been tremendous. I imagine that is the case not so much because I'm that great of a writer of the material but because the material is practical and usable in the real world (vs. esoteric educational material) and because the majority of the topics in the courses are new to those who take them. No other entity in the country provides unbiased education on asset protection, which is the foundation of the three certification courses.

My travel has been severely curtailed since I only put on about a handful of in-person seminars a year; and I get to do what I've found I'm best at, which is to help other advisors fashion solutions for their clients. Therefore, it seems that the move from full-time consulting to educating advisors and working with their clients has turned out to be a good move for me, my family, and those who have taken my courses.

## THE ASSET PROTECTION SOCIETY

As the certification courses continued to get traction nationwide, I was always searching for the next challenge. I found that next challenge when I decided to form a new society called the Asset Protection Society (APS™).

I finally got tired of all the asset-protection "scammers" in the marketplace who were luring unsuspecting clients to do business with them only to have the clients find out that the services they purchased were worthless and usually far too expensive.

I formed the APS™ with a handful of other like-minded advisors with one overriding goal and that was to form an organization that would protect the public.

The APS™ is a place where the public can receive baseline education on how to protect assets from creditors (like the personal injury attorneys I used to work for). In addition, the APS™ "rates" advisors on their knowledge of what I call "global-asset protection."

My definition of global-asset protection is that anyone or anything that can take your money is a creditor. Think about that for a second. Who is your number one creditor every year? The IRS. Is the stock market a creditor? Sure. Did you lose money in the stock market in 2000-2002 when it lost nearly 50% of its value and again in 2007-2008 when it lost 59% of its value? What about the costs of long-term care? Is that an expense that will take your money in retirement? Absolutely.

I wanted to create a Society that would set the "standard of care" in the industry for how to provide asset-protection advice, and I wanted the public to feel comfortable going to the Society to look for help from "rated" advisors. I believe the APS™ is such a place, and I look forward to having it grow over the coming years with the help of all of its members and State Representatives.

If you are interested in asset protection or finding an advisor who can help you, please check out the Society on the web.

## NOT BELIEVING NUMBERS

Since you know I'm an attorney, you've probably already surmised that I am a cynic at heart (especially in the financial services and insurance fields). I do not take someone's word that a product works as it's been touted. Many times what advisors are told about financial/insurance products are half truths. They are the truths that marketing organizations, insurance companies, or broker dealers want advisors to know.

Because of this, I determined that in order for me to help advisors provide the best advice to their clients when it came to financial products, I better figure out a way to crunch the numbers myself.

As it turns out, I'm a numbers junkie. While 99% of the population has no interest in sitting in front of a computer breaking down the math of a financial instrument, I really enjoy it. I enjoy it so much that I have my own programming team that helps me build software applications to further help me break down numbers to come up with the holy grail of conclusions, which is whether the financial product/instrument really functions as touted. I can tell you that the vast majority of the time the answer is NO, which is one of the problems in the financial services/insurance industries.

## EDUCATING AND WARNING ADVISORS

My business grows each year for one main reason: I send weekly educational newsletters out to over 300,000 insurance/financial advisors, CPAs/EAs/accountants, and attorneys.

As it turns out, my educational newsletters are some of, if not, the most well-read newsletters in the financial services/insurance industry. Why? There's one simple reason: I am just about the only one in the industry who devotes significant time in newsletters telling advisors what they are doing wrong, that the products they are selling are not as advertised, and how to avoid scams in the marketplace.

How do I know that specific products/tools are no good or not as advertised? As I stated earlier, I'm the ultimate numbers junkie, and I break the numbers down until I get a yes or no answer about whether products will perform (or the likelihood they will perform) as advertised.

**What you will learn in this book is that most financial planners and life/annuity sales people do not do their own independent research on the various products or concepts they use to help clients. They typically take the word or recommendation of a sales organization and run with products or concepts without doing the needed due diligence to determine if either are good for their clients.**

Also, attorneys and CPAs/EAs/accountants do not have anyone helping them find innovative, new, and/or better ways to help clients (which is one reason the best advice is often not given to clients by these types of advisors).

What's important for you to understand about my weekly newsletters is that they are written in an in-your-face/black-and-white manner where I come off as a bit of a "know it all." That's done on purpose for a few reasons that are unimportant for this book, but the bi-product of sending such newsletters to such a large audience is that every week I have advisors trying to tell me why I'm wrong or try to tell me that they know something I don't.

The feedback I receive from advisors is instrumental in keeping me on top of cutting-edge trends in the financial, insurance, legal, and accounting communities.

**OTHER BOOKS**

In an effort to help tell the truth about two separate marketing schemes in the insurance industry, I published two books: <u>The Home Equity Management Guidebook: How to Achieve Maximum Wealth with Maximum Protection</u> (HEMGB) and <u>The Home Equity Acceleration Plan</u> (H.E.A.P.™).

The HEMGB was written to tell the truth about two of the worst books ever published on how to build wealth (<u>Missed Fortune 101</u> and <u>Stop Sitting on Your Assets</u>). I was so upset at the misinformation in these books that I not only wrote my own book but I put up websites so consumers could read what's wrong with these books. You can find the websites at <u>www.www-missedfortune101.com</u> and <u>www.www-stopsittingonyourassets.com</u>.

I wrote the <u>Home Equity Acceleration Plan</u> book to tell readers about a very unique concept that will help them pay off a mortgage 5-10-15 years early without having to change their lifestyle. I also have a H.E.A.P.™ non-profit where I use the proceeds from the book and accompanying software program to help families who are financially struggling to pay their mortgages.

One of my other books it titled: <u>Retiring Without Risk</u> (RWR). I will refer to the content in RWR several times in this book because in RWR I tell readers about tools to grow wealth that most advisors don't know about or are forbidden from selling.

My most recent book it titled: <u>Peace of Mind Planning: Losing Money is No Longer an Option</u>. I wrote this book to explain investment risk (in the stock market) like I've never seen it explained before. It's difficult to explain in plain English how investment risk works. However, not only do I explain investment risk so anyone can understand it, I also lay out alternative ways to grow money in the stock market with minimal risk. Alternative? To what? To mutual funds, index funds, bonds, stocks, etc.

Would you be interested in an investment that had 70% less volatility than the S&P 500 with better historical returns? I think so, but the problem is that most advisors are not familiar with the use of what I call low drawdown risk/tactically managed strategies.

## THE END

By "the end," I mean the end of my overly long summary of my background. I probably made this section of the book too long; but I figure, if you are not interested in the whole story, you can flip through it or skip it. I know that when I talk with people these days they seem interested in the whole story so I thought I would put it in the book.

The end of the story is really the beginning of this new book, Bad Advisors: How to Identify Them; How to Avoid Them. As you now know, the reason I felt compelled to write this book is because of the bad advice consumers are being given by the vast majority of advisors in various industries. Bad advice from advisors to consumers or consumers having nowhere to turn for good advice has cost millions of Americans billions of dollars.

This book won't solve every American's problems, but I am confident that readers will never look at an advisor the same way and will be armed with knowledge to determine if an advisor is competent or is giving advice that is in the advisor's best interest instead of the reader's.

Until now, most people have no idea if their advisors are good or bad. That ever-nagging question in the back of everyone's mind will be answered one way or another by reading this book.

While the chances are significant that most readers have one or more "bad advisors" and that reading this book can be frightening or even a bit depressing, it should serve as a wakeup call and will arm readers with the knowledge to rid themselves of "bad advisors" and hire ones who are competent and who will provide the best consumer-friendly advice.

Thank you for reading this book; and I hope it helps you avoid "bad advisors," identify "good advisors," and grow and protect your wealth in the least risky/most tax-favorable manner possible.

Roccy M. DeFrancesco, JD, CWPP™, CAPP™, CMP™
Founder: The Wealth Preservation Institute
roccy@badadvisors.com

# <u>Chapter 1</u>

## Everyone's Worst Nightmare

I need to qualify the title of this chapter a bit before I begin. "Everyone" is a pretty broad term. I need to define everyone so this chapter will make sense, and so I can save you time when reading it.

Everyone will NOT include unemployed people with no money. This includes children or young adults in college.

Also, everyone will be broken out into different categories (so you can read the one that applies to you). I'll start with seniors and work backwards.

### What is a "worst nightmare"?

I need to define "worst nightmare" for use in this chapter. The nightmare will be slightly different for different categories of people; but for use in this chapter, the nightmare is when someone receives bad financial, legal, accounting, and/or insurance advice that hurts their ability to retire in the desired manner and pass the maximum amount of wealth to heirs if so desired.

## 80-YEAR OLD WIDOW WITH ASSETS OF LESS THAN $1 MILLION

As you will find out after reading this book, an 80-year old client has already had dozens of "bad advisors" in her life that have led her to have less than $1 million at this age. That nightmare can't be fixed, so I'll focus on the potential nightmare at hand.

If you read the statistics on the elderly, they are a bit depressing. There are 40 million Americans over 65 – 13% of total population. There will be 80 million Americans over 65 by 2040. Eighty percent will require long-term care (LTC) during their lifetime. Fifty percent will require care for a minimum of one year and twenty percent over five years.

Unfortunately, most people do not plan for LTC expenses, and many think that the government through Medicaid will help pay for these expenses.

Here's a classic nightmare situation for an 80-year old client who has less than $1 million in assets. The client has an accountant who does her taxes, an attorney who has drafted estate planning documents (maybe), and a financial planner who is helping manage her liquid assets (either in an IRA or not).

Assume this example client has $300,000 in an IRA and/or brokerage account or CDs or money market accounts.

NONE of her advisors know anything about **Medicaid planning**. NONE of them know that, if and when she goes into a nursing home, she will have to **spend down** virtually all of her assets to **$2,000** (and no that's not a typo) in order to receive financial aid from Medicaid for nursing-home care.

As it turns out, this client is in poor health and will need to go into a nursing home within the next 12 months.

Because she is surrounded by "bad advisors," she will have to spend her entire $300,000 in liquid assets down to $2,000 before she will qualify for Medicaid assistance. With the average private-pay nursing home cost at approximately $5,000 a month, she will spend down her assets in five years.

**IF** this client wasn't surrounded by "bad advisors," she would have been able to plan for the nearly inevitable fact of life which is that she would need to go into a nursing home at some point in her senior life. With proper planning, this example client could have passed some, if not all, of her $300,000 liquid assets to her heirs and still qualified for Medicaid.

**IF** she had a really "good advisor" helping her, even though she did not plan prior to entering a nursing home, it would still be possible to immediately qualify her for aid or design a Medicaid plan for her so that she can qualify for aid in less than a year while giving in excess of $100,000 of her liquid wealth to her heirs (instead of spending it all on nursing home expenses).

**IF** she had a "good advisor" when she was younger, the advisor would have counseled her to buy LTC insurance which would have eliminated the need to spend down her assets to $2,000 prior to qualifying for financial aid from Medicaid.

This classic example is not only a nightmare for the example client, but it is also a nightmare for her heirs. All of this could have been avoided with proper planning by a "good advisor."

## MIDDLE-CLASS, 67-YEAR OLD WHO RETIRED IN 2007

This type of client is your classic baby boomer who has worked hard for years and now is ready to enjoy the fruits of his/her labor.

However, there's a problem. This middle-class American has been using "bad advisors" for years which has put at risk an enjoyable retirement.

I'm going to assume that this example client (Mr. Smith) is married, has three children, and five grandchildren. Assume he had the following assets in **2007**: $400,000 home with little debt, cars that are paid off, and $1,000,000 in his employer's 401(k)/Profit Sharing Plan.

With $1 million in a tax-deferred retirement plan, you'd think it would be no problem for Mr. Smith to retire and never run out of money. Right?

Wrong!

Mr. Smith had a financial planner who worked for a large broker dealer (BD) (you'll learn about BDs later) who had Mr. Smith's IRA money in a "properly balanced stock and mutual fund portfolio."

What happened in 2007? The stock market crashed **59%** from the high of 2007 to the low of 2008.

Therefore, when Mr. Smith decided to retire near the end of 2008, he had a real problem. His retirement account balance was $410,000 instead of $1,000,000.

What's Mr. Smith supposed to do now? No matter what he does, if he starts taking income from his retirement account, the income will be less than 50% of what it would have been if he didn't have a bad financial advisor.

Why was Mr. Smith's advisor a "bad advisor?" There are several reasons I'll get into in future chapters, but the main reason is because Mr. Smith was in the classic "properly balanced stock and mutual fund portfolio."

Mr. Smith should have had some or even all of his money in wealth-building tools that would not go backwards in the event of a stock-market crash.

If Mr. Smith knew about a wealth-building tool that would **guarantee him a 7% rate of return** on an accumulation value coupled with a **lifetime income stream he could never outlive** that would pay him based on a **5.7% income stream** at age 67, do you think he would have been interested in such a tool back in 2007? Do you think a "good advisor" would know about such products and would have made Mr. Smith aware of them?

What will shock you is that such products did (and do) exist and that many "bad advisors" do not know anything about these products or, what's worse, they know about them but are forbidden from selling them or even discussing them with clients (this will be discussed in more detail in an upcoming chapter).

This is the most common scenario I see on a day-to-day basis with the "bad advisors" in the financial services and insurance communities.

The bottom line for this client is that, because he had a "bad advisor," he will have to decide if he can afford to retire; or if he does choose to retire, he will have to change his retirement lifestyle. It's a real shame, but there are millions of Americans who have and who will face this situation; and it all could be avoided by using a "good advisor."

## 65-YEAR OLD MULTI-MILLIONAIRE

Today, being a multi-millionaire is not as tough as it sounds. While the real estate market has taken a hit, there are many people with $500,000 houses and many other assets (including life insurance proceeds) that when added up push clients over the $2,000,000 mark.

Here are the assumptions for this Dr. Smith example. He is a solo doctor in his own medical practice that generates a net profit each year of $250,000 (his pre-tax, take-home pay). He has the following assets: $750,000 home, $1,000,000 in a tax-deferred retirement plan, a commercial building with little debt (used for the business) worth $500,000, he and his wife have permanent life insurance policies with a $1,000,000 death benefit each, and a brokerage account of $250,000.

He owns his brokerage account and the commercial property **in his own name**. The life insurance policies are owned in the name of each spouse.

If you add it all up, his taxable estate is $4.5 million. Dr. Smith is married and has two children and four grandchildren. His goal is to retire in a few years and **never run out of money in retirement**. He is worried about lawsuits from patients, downturns in the stock market, and paying estate taxes and other fees upon his death.

His attorney set up wills and revocable living trusts only but did NOT fund them.

His financial planner has his liquid wealth in a "properly balanced stock and mutual fund portfolio."

His CPA simply processes his tax returns each year and does not give any real tax advice.

His insurance agent sold him the life insurance policies 10 years ago, and he has not seen him since.

What are the problems that have been created by his "bad advisors?"

Bad advice from the **Attorney**

1) Neither Dr. Smith nor his wife has medical or legal powers of attorney. These are vital in any estate plan to make sure the healthy spouse doesn't have to go to court to make life-sustaining decisions or be authorized to make financial decisions for the incapacitated spouse.

2) The revocable living trusts are not funded. Unfunded trusts will cause his estate to be probated which will cause tremendous headaches and expense for his heirs. This is a classic error many estate-planning attorneys make, which will be discussed in an upcoming chapter.

3) The life insurance policies should be in an Irrevocable Life Insurance Trust (ILIT). Without the policies in an ILIT, the death benefit will be subject to estate taxes at the second spouse's death (which after 2011 could cost the heirs upwards of 55% of the benefit). Once the life insurance is in an ILIT, Dr. Smith's estate will be $2.5 million; and with proper structuring, no estate taxes should be due when the last remaining spouse dies.

4) The commercial building should be in a multi-member LLC. Without the building in an LLC, Dr. Smith's other assets are at risk to the liability of the building. Additionally, Dr. Smith could be saving on income taxes by paying rent to the LLC from the medical practice (which is unearned income and better from an income-tax perspective than earned income or W-2 income).

5) The brokerage account should also be in a multi-member LLC for asset-protection purposes. This brokerage account is at risk to lawsuits from Dr. Smith's patients or from any negligence lawsuit (like from an auto accident).

Bad advice from the **CPA**

1) The commercial building should be in a multi-member LLC for the same reasons stated in the attorney section.

This is the main issue most people would gripe about to the CPA (because the client could be paying rent to the LLC that owns the building and saving on income taxes). However, I believe that a good CPA should also offer estate-planning advice such as telling the client he needs durable powers of attorney, needs to fund his trusts, and needs to move his and his wife's life insurance policies into an ILIT to minimize estate taxes.

While it's rare for a CPA to know anything about asset protection, it would be nice if the CPA could also counsel the client on this very important subject matter.

Some CPAs attempt to offer financial planning and insurance advice, and I'll assume in this example that is not the case. I will address CPAs offering these services in a future chapter.

Bad advice from the **Financial Planner**

1) Allowing Dr. Smith, who is fearful of losing money in the stock market and who would like to retire and not worry about running out of money, to remain in a "properly balanced stock and mutual fund portfolio" is a classic error.

What I didn't state in the fact pattern is that Dr. Smith **used to have** nearly $2,000,000 in his qualified retirement plan prior to the stock-market crash of 2007-2008.

A good financial planner would have slowly transitioned Dr. Smith's money to more conservative investments or to a product that would guarantee a rate of return coupled with a guaranteed income for life.

2) Allowing Dr. Smith's estate-planning documents to remain incomplete—many financial planners tout themselves not just as stock pickers but as full-service advisors who know estate planning as well (Certified Financial Planners (CFPs®) are notorious for touting these additional benefits).

Like the attorney, the financial planner should have recommended that Dr. Smith's revocable-living trusts get funded, that he and his wife obtain durable powers of attorney, and especially that the life insurance policies should be transferred to an ILIT.

If a financial planner or CFP® is touting comprehensive services, he/she should also give counsel on asset protection as well; but I can tell you for a fact that is an unrealistic expectation.

Bad advice from the **Insurance Agent**

In this fact pattern, there really isn't an insurance agent. The agent sold Dr. Smith and his wife policies 10 years ago, and they have not heard from the agent since.

If a new insurance agent came into the picture, he/she should, at the very least, address:

1) That the life policies should be moved into ILITs.

2) That the money in both the qualified plan and the brokerage account are at risk in the stock market and that other tools should be looked at to grow wealth in a manner consistent with the client's goals and objectives (no risk of loss and an income that cannot be outlived).

3) The agent should also discuss the various ways to purchase LTC insurance or receive a free LTC benefit with a life or annuity product.

Again, while it would be nice if an insurance agent knew something about asset protection, corporate structure, etc., that is not the case with the vast majority of advisors in the insurance industry.

At first glance, this example client's situation seemed fairly simple. You can see it took a whole team of "bad advisors" to allow Dr. Smith's assets to be at risk in the stock market, put his assets at risk to the probate fees and the probate process, subject his and his wife's life insurance proceeds to estate taxes, allow nearly all of his personal assets to be at risk to negligence lawsuits, have one spouse be forced to go to court in the event the other spouse becomes incapacitated, and so on and so on.

## MIDDLE-CLASS, 45-YEAR OLD

There are millions of middle-class working folk that deserve better advice than they are receiving.

In this example, assume Mr. Smith is married and has two teenage children. He and his spouse work and earn $110,000 a year as their pre-tax pay. They have a house worth $300,000 with $200,000 in debt on it. Both have new jobs and each has $100,000 in roll-over IRAs that are managed by their accountant who also has his securities and life insurance license. The IRA money is in variable annuities.

They have a rental property that is in Mr. Smith's name. Mr. Smith has a whole life insurance policy with a $500,000 death benefit that was sold to him by his State Farm agent with a $2,500-a-year premium (who keeps trying to get him to pay more premiums into the policy each year and to use the policy as a wealth-building tool).

Both children plan to go to college, and the parents are going to help pay for it (although they'd like the children to receive financial aid). After expenses, the couple could save $10,000 a year (although they usually find a way to spend it).

They have not done their estate plan yet.

### Bad advice from the **Attorney**

They don't have an attorney at this point in time so no bad advice is being given. When they find one, hopefully the attorney will help them implement wills, revocable living trusts (which should be funded), and durable powers of attorney.

### Bad advice from the **CPA**

Mr. Smith doesn't have a CPA; he has an accountant who charges him $125 to process his tax return each year. Assuming the accountant is competent, he/she is doing about all that is typically expected out of him/her (so no bad advice is being given).

However, for this example, assume the accountant is also offering investment advisory services.

### Bad advice from the **Financial Planner**

As stated, the accountant is also the client's financial planner and is managing the money in the couple's IRAs. The accountant has the client's money in variable annuities (VAs). As you'll find out in an upcoming chapter, most CPAs/accountants/EAs who are offering financial planning have no idea what they are doing and are relying on others to help them provide advice to their clients.

Tax-deferred variable annuities are very fee-heavy products that are generally not sold in tax-deferred IRAs. If they are, the reason is because the product has a guaranteed income rider. Most VAs have fees in excess of 2.5% a year. Inside a VA, clients will typically invest their money in a limited selection of mutual funds.

While clients of this age should have a certain amount of their money in the stock market, again, generally speaking, it is not a good idea to buy a VA inside an IRA. The expense is too great; and if the client is interested in a guaranteed income rider, the fixed indexed annuities in the marketplace are far superior (as you'll learn in an upcoming chapter).

While the Smiths are on the edge of being too young, they may be candidates for a fixed-indexed annuity that will guarantee an 8% rate of return for up to 20 years with a guaranteed income for life based on a 5% income percentage in retirement starting at age 65. Using such a product would guarantee that their combined $200,000 in qualified-plan assets would grow to $949,454 and would then be used to guarantee a retirement income of $51,271 every year for life.

As their financial planner, he/she should have discussed with the Smiths whether it makes financial sense to fund their tax-deferred 401(k) plan at work. As you will learn, tax-deferred plans can be more tax-hostile than tax-favorable; and at their age, there can be better ways to grow a tax-favorable retirement nest egg.

As the couple's financial planner, the accountant should also be addressing their life insurance needs. The whole life policy from State Farm should be reviewed, and the couple should be warned that they are underinsured. However, I'm going to make my example typical of the industry; and I'll assume that the accountant, even though he has his life insurance license, doesn't know much about it and chooses not to give advice about the client being underinsured and whether the State Farm policy is any good.

Finally, because a financial planner can and should sell LTC insurance and because the Smiths do not have it, the accountant/agent should have educated them on the value and need for LTC insurance and advocated that they purchase a policy on both Mr. and Mrs. Smith. At their ages, it would be fairly inexpensive.

Bad advice from the **Insurance Agent**

The first problem is that the client has chosen to buy life insurance from a State Farm agent. You'll learn why in detail in an upcoming chapter.

Assume that the State Farm agent sold the client the same product he tries to sell everyone which is the company's primary whole life policy. This policy was sold as a cash-accumulation vehicle because money can grow tax-free and come out tax-free from a life policy. This can work out very well IF you choose the "right" life insurance policy.

In my example, I want you to assume that the State Farm whole life policy is not one of the better policies in the market; but it is the one that the State Farm agent chose to offer Mr. Smith. Because Mr. Smith didn't know any better and because alternative types of policies from multiple companies were not offered, he ended up buying the State Farm policy.

Additionally, the State Farm agent did not properly counsel/educate the Smiths on the real power of growing wealth using cash value life insurance as a wealth-building tool. The agent in my example does not understand the math of using a "good" cash value life insurance policy as a tax-favorable/wealth-building tool. For a 45-year old such as Mr. Smith, the math supports funding a "good" policy over a tax-deferred qualified plan (to learn the math behind using cash value life insurance as a wealth-building tool, see my book <u>Retiring Without Risk</u>).

Besides selling Mr. Smith an inferior life insurance product and not properly educating on the value of a "good" cash value life insurance policy as a tax-favorable/wealth-accumulation tool, the agent did not inform Mr. and Mrs. Smith that they are underinsured. The $500,000 death benefit is not enough to care for Mrs. Smith and pay for the children's education if he should happen to die. While Mrs. Smith is employed, Mr. Smith makes slightly more money; and their lifestyle is predicated on a dual household income.

Also, because a life insurance agent sells life insurance for estate-planning purposes, it would have been proper for the agent to tell the Smiths that their estate-planning documents are not in order.

Finally, because a life insurance agent can and should sell LTC insurance and because the Smiths do not have it, the agent should have educated them on the value and need for LTC insurance and advocated that they purchase a policy on both Mr. and Mrs. Smith. At their ages, it would be fairly inexpensive.

### **Miscellaneous advice for the Smiths**

The average attorney, CPA, financial planner, or insurance agent will give certain advice that we all expect (it might not be any good, but they try to give it).

There are other issues that the Smiths might want to get help with.

1) Paying down the mortgage on their home. Most advisors do not know of a program like the Home Equity Acceleration Plan (H.E.A.P.™) (www.heaplan.com). This is a very unique plan that helps clients pay down their mortgage 5-10-15 years early without having to change their lifestyle. It would have been a welcome subject matter to discuss if one of the Smith's advisors would have brought it up.

2) College planning. Because the Smith's children are already teenagers, there is no magic wand over paying for their children's college education. The Smiths have been given no college planning advice over the years by any of their advisors which is why they have not saved for it.

While I don't have any magic advice to fund their children's college education, I would warn them to be careful of paying for advice from a so called "college planning specialist." As you'll find out, there are many advisors parading around as "college planners" as a marketing ploy. Needless to say, most of the advice given by these advisors is bad advice; and I'll discuss this in more detail in an upcoming chapter.

## 30-YEAR OLD WHO JUST GOT MARRIED

It seems that many younger Americans are getting married later in life. For this example, assume the Smiths just got married and have no children. They both work and have no immediate plans to have children. Each makes $50,000 a year.

They have no wills, trusts, or durable powers. They have no life insurance. They have no savings. They just bought a house worth $250,000 with $200,000 of debt (their parents both gave them the additional money they needed to make the $50,000 down payment).

They don't know what they should be doing or who they should be talking with to receive unbiased advice to get their estate plan in order and to start building wealth for retirement.

There is no need to identify the Smiths' "bad advisors" because they don't have any advisors right now. It will be key for the Smiths to surround themselves with "good advisors" so they can get their estate and financial affairs in order.

The best thing the Smiths can do is read this book and use the content to help them find good advisors they can work with.

### SUMMARY ABOUT NIGHTMARES

The few fact patterns I've chosen to discuss in this chapter are the common/plain vanilla ones I see quite often.

Believe it or not, these stories are NOT anywhere close to the most egregious situations I've run across.

My point with this chapter is to peak the average reader's interest. My guess is that, if you are 45-years and older and have read this chapter, you can identify with some of the bad advice that's been given to my example clients.

If you are under the age of 45 and have done no planning, hopefully this chapter has sufficiently motivated you to read on so you can learn how to avoid "bad advisors" when it comes time to choose your own.

# Chapter 2

## Insurance Marketing Organizations

Why am I starting this book with an early chapter on Insurance Marketing Organizations (IMOs)?

Mainly because I need to give you background information on what really drives a good portion of the life insurance and annuity sales made in the industry. Learning about IMOs will help you understand why there is so much bad advice being given when it comes to sales of fixed life insurance and annuities.

This chapter is a look into the insurance industry that no insurance agent will tell you about. I consider this chapter a **dirty little secrets chapter** where I will give you valuable insight you will not receive anywhere else.

I also need to qualify the term "**fixed**" as it is used in conjunction with life insurance and annuities. Fixed life insurance and annuities by definition are not "**variable**." To sell a fixed life insurance policy or a fixed annuity, you only need a life insurance license. To sell a variable annuity or variable life insurance policy, you need a securities license.

Variable products will be dealt with in the chapters on Broker Dealers and Securities Licensed Advisors.

### WHAT IS A GENERAL AGENT (GA)?

If this chapter is about IMOs, why am I discussing GAs? GAs were the predecessor to what we in the industry call IMOs. IMOs are also known in the industry as FMOs (field marketing organizations).

A GA is a person or more typically an entity that "in the old days" used to recruit insurance agents to sell products.

What do I mean when I say recruit? Through various marketing efforts, GAs would try to find potential advisors (not licensed yet) and currently licensed agents to sell life insurance and annuities through the GA.

How did they recruit? If they wanted to recruit new agents and bring them into the business, some GAs would go to college campuses. Some would advertise in various journals and papers, and some would recruit through word of mouth.

What was the sales pitch to a not-yet licensed advisor? The GA would tout that it offered education/training on the products that will be sold; and that, once trained, the agents could make significant money selling life insurance and annuity products.

Some GAs would offer a **minimal salary** for a period of time (which was more like an advance or draw), **health insurance**, and **office space** (or an office allowance). If the recruited agent did well, the money put out up front by the GA would be recouped from future commissions generated by the agent.

How do GAs make money? They make an override commission on all business placed by recruited agents.

For example, if a newly licensed insurance agent sold a product that paid a $1,000 commission, the GA would make an override of between $400-$500 or more. If a more seasoned agent sells the same product, the override would be between $200-$400.

The business model of a GA is fairly simple—recruit as many good insurance sales people as possible so the maximum amount of overrides can be generated. Once built, it's a terrific recurring revenue model for the GA.

### Captive and independent GAs

GAs can be either captive or independent. A captive GA is one who recruits only for one particular life insurance company (like Guardian). An independent GA is one who can represent multiple insurance companies. I'll give you my very negative opinion on captive GAs/IMOs later in this chapter.

### Why were GAs needed?

Why don't insurance agents simply go directly to insurance companies and sign up to sell their products? There are several reasons, but the two main ones are: 1) the ability to maximize compensation of the agent is less; 2) many insurance companies did not want to put effort and money into recruiting and training.

Way back in the day (and still true for a few companies today), insurance companies actually did their own recruiting and training. Over time, recruiting and training was outsourced to GAs who, again, recruited for one company in particular or for a handful of companies.

### GAs are a dying breed

Today, GAs are going the way of the dinosaur. They are slowly becoming extinct.

Why? Because the GA model is a greedy override model. Back in the day, the mentality of a new insurance agent was that they would essentially be employees of the GA. That is not technically accurate in most cases because the insurance agent was an independent contractor.

However, the sales pitch again was that the agent coming on board would be given money so the agent could afford to live until his/her sales started coming in and that the agent would be provided health insurance and be given office space or an office allowance.

When a better model came out (the IMO model) that could pay agents more or significantly more money, over time the industry has shifted away from the low agent compensation model of GAs and has shifted to the more flexible and higher paying IMO model.

### WHAT IS AN INDEPENDENT MARKETING ORGANIZATION (IMO)?

As you'll find out, the term "independent" in IMO is, for the most part, a misnomer (most IMOs are not "independent").

An IMO is a company that recruits insurance agents to sell fixed life insurance and annuity products.

It sounds like a GA, right? It's similar, but IMOs do not provide health insurance; and they do not provide office space or office allowances.

IMOs tout that they provide training; but for 95% of the IMOs in the industry, that is not the case.

IMOs are **supposed to be independent**. They are supposed to help insurance agents sell products through multiple insurance companies (vs. one company or only a handful of companies like old-school GAs).

Because IMOs do not provide health insurance, office space, or an office allowance and because most spend little or no money on training, the IMO can afford to pay insurance agents higher commissions.

Why were IMOs formed, and why are they still in existence?

Ironically, the early IMOs were formed by insurance companies to fill the growing void. What void? Many insurance companies were getting away from allocating money to training and educating advisors on products. IMOs were formed as third-party educators on products sold by insurance companies.

While that was a novel idea, over time, many IMOs were created to help insurance agents maximize commissions (this was not the case with GAs who paid low commission rates because of their higher expenses per agent).

I asked the following question earlier: Why don't most insurance agents get contracted directly through insurance companies instead of through a GA or IMO?

Today the answer is **MONEY**. Think about it. If an insurance agent goes to insurance company XZY and says he/she can place $1,000,000 in annuity business a year, does that allow the agent an ability to negotiate a high commission arrangement? The answer is an emphatic NO!

However, what if an IMO contracts 100 agents who all can place $1,000,000 in annuity business? That's $100 million of annuity premiums. Could an IMO then go to the insurance company and negotiate a higher payout? Absolutely. Then can the IMO, in turn, give a higher commission payout to the agent and still make good money for the IMO? Absolutely.

Agents working through sizable IMOs can earn an additional 10-40% in commissions per product sold.

Therefore, when a sizable IMO recruits an insurance agent, does the IMO have an advantage over insurance companies who try to recruit direct? Absolutely.

Let me get back to the word "**independent**." IMOs are supposed to allow agents to be more independent. Why? Because an IMO might have contracts with 20-30 and even up to 200 different companies. The average agent on the street might be able to obtain contracts at 2-5 companies.

It will be impossible for an agent to get contracted with 20-30+ companies. The companies limit who is contracted because there is an expense per agent. Also, if you are not producing, the insurance companies will eventually terminate you.

In my opinion, in order to give clients the best advice, you have to have access to "all" the reputable companies. IMOs do give agents the best opportunity to have access to all the best products even though most IMOs do not help agents give the best advice (as you'll learn).

I did want to point out the main benefit of working with an agent who works with a good IMO. If the IMO has sufficient clout with an insurance company because of the volume of business placed, the IMO can many times twist the arm of the insurance company when it comes to underwriting for life insurance. Many times I've seen IMOs negotiate the underwriting of a policy from substandard health to standard or from standard to preferred. This may not sound like a big deal, but a better underwriting class has a huge impact on the cost of insurance and can be the determining factor as to whether a consumer buys a policy or not.

**Insurance company recruiting is dead**

IMOs have such a foothold in the industry that many insurance companies no longer try to actively recruit insurance agents directly to the company.

Over time, the percentage of business placed through IMOs in the industry is at such a high percentage that IMOs are the entities in our industry that drive what products are sold.

This has created sort of a love-hate relationship between IMOs and the insurance companies they represent. As IMOs have gotten bigger, they have become more demanding on insurance companies. As you can imagine, IMOs have been flexing their muscles and have tried to strong arm insurance companies into paying more and more override commissions to the IMO.

Insurance companies for a long period of time went along with this model which did nothing but fuel the creation of more and bigger IMOs.

Interestingly, IMOs have recently become too greedy and too demanding. As profits have been shrinking at many insurance companies due to poor stock market performance, they have pushed back a bit.

Some insurance companies have even terminated contracts with a few very large IMOs. Why? Because insurance companies have been pushing for more loyalty from IMOs, and ones that were terminated were doing some production but not enough production to keep the very high commission override contracts that had been negotiated.

## WHY MOST IMOs ARE NOT GOOD FOR THE INDUSTRY OR CONSUMER

I'm not sure if you noticed but when I explained why IMOs were formed I did not say they were formed for the benefit of the consumer who ends up purchasing a life or annuity product.

IMOs were formed so IMO owners could make money and so agents could make more money. The theory was that agents could offer more products to clients by working through an IMO that has access to 20-30-100-200 companies, but the reality is that most IMOs do not help agents provide the best advice to their clients.

Why?

I'll give you one guess. **MONEY**.

Think about it. If an IMO does its job in helping licensed agents find the best product for each individual client, that would create a situation where premium dollars that flow through the IMO really will get spread out among many different insurance companies.

If the IMO spreads premium dollars among many different companies, what happens to the negotiating power of the IMO to demand higher commissions from the insurance companies it represents? It drops like a stone.

Therefore, guess what happens in the real world when "most" IMOs recommend products? They end up recommending the same products over and over and over. By doing so, they assure that the IMO will meet certain production marks with certain insurance companies.

Guess what happens when an IMO meets certain production marks with an insurance company? If you're following the theme of this chapter, you'll know the answer is that the IMO makes **MORE MONEY**. IMOs make millions of dollars each year by reaching various production levels and are provided cash bonuses when they reach them.

### Independent?

Unfortunately, most insurance agents have no idea of the games that are played internally at IMOs. Most insurance agents are sold a bill of goods by an IMO that the IMO has "top contracts" at all the major insurance companies. Therefore, if the agent works with the IMO, the internal staff at the IMO will make sure the agents receive recommendations that are best for their clients.

Unfortunately, that is not the reality of the industry.

Let me digress for a bit to tell you how IMOs work with insurance agents. Once insurance agents decide to get contracted through an IMO with 1-5-10+ different insurance companies, they are assigned a life insurance marketer and an annuity marketer.

Marketers sit in a cubicle all day answering e-mails and phone calls from insurance agents who are looking to sell products to their clients.

Let me go through an example of what is supposed to happen when an insurance agent calls an IMO for help with a specific client.

The agent calls his/her marketer at the IMO and says that his/her client is 65-years old, is about to retire, and would like a product that would guarantee a rate of return coupled with a guaranteed income for life.

The marketer says, "Great. Let me get a little more information." Then the marketer will recommend 1-2 products for the agent to choose from.

The marketer is supposed to have the knowledge of "all" the useable products and be able to make an "unbiased" recommendation to the agent.

The agent picks product one and sells it to his/her client and thinks he/she received great service from the IMO.

Let me tell you the problems with IMO marketers:

1) Many of them don't fully understand the products they are recommending. This obviously makes it impossible for the best products to be recommended to the agent.

2) Many of them do not know all the available products. This is because many marketers get used to the same 1-2-3 products and are not professional enough to make sure they spend a significant amount of their time researching the frequent changes to products in the market and the new ones that come out. Again, this makes it impossible for a marketer to recommend the best products to the agent.

3) Most marketers are paid a percentage of the commission override on cases sold. Why is this a problem? **GREED!** I can't tell you the number of conversations I've had with marketers over the years where they've told me they push one product over another because the commission override for them is better (no, the commission for the insurance agent selling the product isn't any better).

Yes, this is outrageous and is one of the reasons I decided to write this book.

4) Most IMOs do not really have access to "all" the available products. Most IMOs are small or medium sized, and they simply don't have contracts with all the companies they need to in order for marketers and agents to have access to the "best" products.

There are a handful of very large IMOs who have access to just about any independently sold products, but they are a minority in the industry (and it wouldn't matter most of the time because the marketers are still going to recommend their 1-2-3 core products to agents because the agent won't know any better and because the compensation for the marketer is higher).

Is this starting to crystallize for you?

The vast majority of "independent" insurance advisors selling products do so through IMOs. The agents are relying on IMOs to help them pick the best products for their clients.

Unfortunately, most agents are selling products through IMOs that don't have access to all the best products.

Unfortunately, most agents are dealing with marketers who couldn't pick the best product for their client if it were sitting in front of them with a blinking red light (because most marketers are incompetent).

Unfortunately, even if the marketer helping the agent giving advice is competent, the chances are significant that your agent is still not going to be given the best products to offer you because the one with the highest commission override instead is going to be recommended.

If you are sitting there thinking that **your** insurance agent just happens to be the one who is working with an IMO that has all the needed contracts, that has a competent staff of marketers, who will recommend the best products, and ignore how much money can be made by recommending an inferior product, **you're living in a fantasy world**.

### SOME IMOs ARE OWNED BY INSURANCE COMPANIES!

If what I've told you already doesn't put doubt in your mind about an insurance agent's ability to provide you with the best products, I wanted to let you know that many IMOs in the insurance industry are **partially owned by insurance companies**.

If you read books like I do, when you read something that is unbelievable or outrageous, you probably just dropped the book on the floor, did a double or triple take at what you just read, or you just readjusted your glasses or rubbed your contacts to make sure what you read said just what you thought it said.

I'm not kidding. There are many IMOs in the insurance business that are partially or are wholly owned by insurance companies.

If it weren't so pathetic, it would be laughable. Have you ever heard of the saying, "having the wolves guard the hen house"? I think that analogy is right on the mark when it comes to having an IMO that is owned by an insurance company give "independent" advice to insurance agents (it's not going to happen).

You don't have to be a genius to follow the bouncing ball on this one. What products do you think get preferential treatment at an IMO that is owned in part or in whole by an insurance company? You're right—the products of the insurance company with an ownership interest.

Are the products from that one company always or even most often the "best" products for all of an insurance agent's clients? The question actually makes me laugh out loud. Of course not.

Do you think the IMO that is partially or wholly owned by an insurance company discloses this to the insurance advisors it recruits? The answer is no.

This illustrates a significant issue in the insurance community. Insurance agents do not make a habit of being in the know and doing their own independent research on products or the IMOs they deal with.

### A hopeless picture?

What are the odds that the agent who sold you your last life insurance policy (term, whole, universal, or indexed) or annuity (fixed, deferred, fixed indexed, etc.) works with an IMO that **can't possibly** provide the agent with the best products?

If you were working with an "independent" insurance advisor, I'd say the odds are in excess of 80%. That means, in my opinion, you have less than a 20% chance of working with an agent who is working with an IMO that gives that agent a chance to provide you the best products (I said a chance because the actual percentage is less due to other issues I'll discuss in other chapters).

**Are you sick to your stomach yet?**

What I've disclosed to you in this chapter 50% or more of the insurance agents selling products don't even know.

Most IMOs are set up by design to NOT provide insurance advisors with the best life insurance and annuity products. Because of this, you should be sick to your stomach.

If you are receiving advice from what I call a "captive" agent (see Chapter 3), the chances are virtually zero that you will be offered the best products for your particular situation. Then you'll really be sick to your stomach.

**Full disclosure**

Why do I know so much about IMOs? Several reasons. First and foremost, I dedicate myself every day to learning as much as I can about the insurance industry in general and specifically the products offered to make sure when I educate advisors I am providing them with the best information.

Why do I really know the GA/IMO structures?

As I indicated in my bio section, I am life and annuity licensed. I used to have real clients before I decided to take my research and knowledge and put it to use to help advisors through The Wealth Preservation Institute.

Over 10 years ago when I obtained my insurance licenses, I **unfortunately** got licensed through an old school GA out of Indiana by the name of Tom Dyer. He was recommended to me by a good friend, and so I made the incorrect assumption that Tom would treat me fairly when it came to commissions. He was your classic GA, and I was your classic newbie to the industry who didn't know anything about contracting and compensation.

I used to market myself exclusively to physicians. This made sense since I wrote a book called The Doctor's Wealth Preservation Guide.

I didn't look to my GA to educate me on products. I did my own detailed research. I didn't look to my GA to help me understand the use of cash value life insurance as a wealth-building tool.

I had no problem finding a handful of clients each year who wanted to buy insurance and/or annuities from me. Since I didn't know anything about contracting and the GA was recommended to me by a friend of mine, I just signed the contracts that were put in front of me so I could sell products I recommended to various clients. I didn't know anything about commissions, and I assumed incorrectly that I would be treated fairly.

Again, I wasn't concerned about selling the best products to my clients because I did my own research to make sure that was the case.

After placing a few life cases through the GA, I found out why life insurance agents like the industry. The money wasn't bad (and keep in mind that, when I sold my first policies, I was actually fully employed at the time and running a five-doctor orthopedic clinic (meaning that I didn't rely on the life commissions to earn a living)).

After continuing to do my research on life and annuity products, I ended up interacting with many different insurance agents. Like employees in a small employer setting who sit around and discuss what each other earns, insurance agents like to sit around and discuss/brag about what they make.

What I found out was that I was in a "career system" under the GA with whom I was working. The career system is one where agents are provided health insurance, office space or an office allowance, and where the ultimate commission to the agent is far less than an independent channel.

I had health insurance and an office through my orthopedic-clinic employer. I didn't look to my GA for support on anything. But what I found out was that I was paid significantly less than I should have been on the life policies I sold. Why?

Because the GA I worked with put me on a beginner's compensation schedule even though I was doing all the work on advanced life insurance sales.

The day I realized that is the day that I decided to become an expert in the flow of money in the insurance business (from insurance company to IMO/FMO/GA to the insurance agent).

### More full disclosure

As I've stated, I send educational newsletters out to over 300,000 life insurance licensed agents. I have also educated hundreds of advisors through in-person seminars over the years. I have also created dozens of marketing tools advisors can use to educate and communicate the value of life and annuity products to their clients.

My point is that there are a lot of insurance advisors who value what I do and who call me for help on case design, products, tax, estate, asset-protection planning, etc.

One question I didn't expect to receive years ago when I started what I do is now one of my more frequent questions. That question is what IMO do I recommend?

As you can tell from reading this chapter, I have significant disdain for IMO/FMOs and GAs. I've dealt with many of them over the years; and three years ago, I actually started looking for one I could work with.

I once tried to form a deal with an IMO to refer agents who wanted me to refer them to an IMO I thought would do a good job. It was a massive failure because the IMO I worked with was woefully understaffed and could not support the agents referred in a manner I wanted them supported.

However, in the fall of 2009, by pure accident, I ended up finding an IMO I could work with. I received a call from the president of the IMO who asked me if I would come speak at his IMO's annual agent convention.

I was quite taken aback by the question. I asked the president if he had read my newsletters over the years and understood my attitude about IMOs (which is that I loathe them). He said he fully understood my disdain for IMOs, and that's why he wanted me to come speak. He asked me to speak on whatever topic I wanted and encouraged me to give my opinion on any subject I wanted to discuss including my thoughts about the industry in general and IMOs specifically.

To make a long story short, after doing several months of due diligence on the IMO, I ended up cutting a referral deal with the IMO. Now when an insurance agent asks me for a referral to an IMO, I have one I can confidently recommend. And, yes, I give full disclosure to the advisor that I will get paid if the advisor places business with the IMO.

Part of my deal with the IMO I work with is that, at any time advisors I recommend to the IMO desire, they can always call me to second guess the advice/recommendation given to them by a marketer at the IMO. Instead of being offended by this, the IMO I work with welcomes my second guessing as a way to help the marketers learn to do a better job and to make sure the agent is provided the very best products possible (and, by the way, I also learn from the marketers through my interaction with them which also helps me continue to improve what I do).

So that's the not-so-short explanation as to why I know so much about IMOs/FMOs/GAs, the compensation structure, and what really happens on a day-to-day basis within an IMO.

## QUESTIONS TO ASK YOUR AGENTS TO DETERMINE IF THEY ARE "BAD ADVISORS"

The following questions are simple and will let you know if your agent is working with an IMO that gives the agent a chance to provide you the best products for your individual situation.

1) Do you work with an IMO, FMO, or GA?

If the agent doesn't know the answer to this question, just hang up the phone or walk out of the meeting. An agent who doesn't know the answer to this question is clueless and should not be used.

If the agent says they work through a GA, know that the chances go down dramatically that he/she is working with a firm that can provide the best products.

2) Is the IMO you work with owned by an insurance company?

I'm not expecting your insurance advisor to know the answer to this even though he/she should. If it were me, that would be enough to show the agent the door; but if you'd like to give the agent a shot, allow him/her to call the IMO and ask (or you can call or e-mail me; and I'll look the IMO up on my list, and I'll tell you). If the answer is that the IMO is owned in part or in full by an insurance company, you are working with a "bad advisor" (or with a pretty bad one who is working with an IMO that can't possibly provide access to the best products).

3) How long has the marketer(s) the agent works with been in the industry?

If the answer is less than two years, the chances that the marketer is not proficient in his/her trade (meaning the chances that the marketer understands the products he/she is recommending and why one is better for a particular client than another) is significant.

4) This is not a question so much to do with IMOs, but you need to make sure to ask your advisor if he/she is "captive."

If your agent is captive, he/she isn't even attempting to work through an independent channel; and, as such, it would be an accident or miracle if the agent provided you with the best products for your particular situation. Even though the independent channel is flawed, you'll be infinitely better off working with an independent agent vs. a captive agent.

# Chapter 3
## Life Insurance/Annuity Agents

I could write an entire 250-page book on "bad" insurance agents. I think the information in such a book would be very helpful to readers; however, it would be overkill and is not really necessary to help readers identify an insurance agent that I would consider a "bad advisor."

Therefore, this chapter will focus on a few specific types of insurance agents and the information about these agents will be all you need to determine if you are dealing with a "bad advisor."

In this chapter I will expose to readers something that most already know and that many, for some odd reason, choose to ignore. Ignore what? That there are many insurance advisors who can only sell products offered by one particular insurance company, i.e., the one the agent works for.

This chapter may seem somewhat similar to the chapter on Broker Dealers (BDs) and "bad" securities licensed advisors. In that upcoming chapter, I discuss how many BDs tie the hands of their advisors by only allowing them to sell certain products (or by strictly forbidding them from selling certain products).

As you will learn in the BD chapter, some BDs forbid their advisors from selling Fixed Indexed Annuities (FIAs) and/or Equity Indexed Universal Life (EIUL) insurance. As you will learn in this chapter, many of those same BDs employ captive insurance agents who are bound by the same restrictive policies when it comes to what products they can sell.

### TWO TYPES OF CAPTIVE AGENTS

I've found that there are two types of captive insurance agents:

1) Contractually captive

2) Mentally captive

Both can be "bad advisors" as you will see.

# WHAT IS A CONTRACTUALLY CAPTIVE ADVISOR?

He/she is an employee of an insurance company. A good example is State Farm.

State Farm advisors are employees of the company and have certain rules they have to follow. If they don't follow the rules, they can have their contracts terminated.

Contractually, captive agents have to sell the products and only the products offered by the company they work for.

For example: If you go to a State Farm agent and ask for a term life insurance quote, guess what you get? That's right—a life insurance quote for a life insurance policy written by State Farm. It is a State Farm product.

If you went to an "independent" insurance agent, the agent should be able to shop your insurance with a number of different companies in order to provide you choices and hopefully the "best" product to fit your particular situation (which also means that many times you will be able to find a product with the lowest possible cost).

## CHANCES OF RECEIVING THE "BEST" ADVICE

Let me ask you a simple question: Do you think you have a better opportunity to receive the "best" advice or products from a captive agent who can ONLY sell you products offered by the company the agent works for, or is it more likely that you'll be able to receive the "best" advice/products from an INDEPENDENT agent who can sell you products from dozens or even hundreds of different companies?

The question is basically a rhetorical one. Of course the chances are much more significant that someone will receive better advice and a better product by working with an independent agent.

Is it possible that once in a blue moon a captive agent will have the "best" product for an individual client? It's possible but very unlikely.

## COMPETING FOR BUSINESS

Are the products offered by captive insurance advisors inferior to those offered by companies that work with independent advisors?

Good question and wouldn't you know it—the answer will depend on whom you ask.

If you ask agents who work for a captive company, they will give you the party line which goes something like this: Our company is financially stable and has had a history of standing behind its products for 100+ years. Our company and our products stand the test of time.

My response is typically yes. I understand that your company has been around for a long time; however, the question was: Does your company offer what can arguably and mathematically be called the "best" products in the industry?

If you receive an honest answer to the question by a captive agent, it will go something like: **I really have no idea if our products are competitive. I'm not allowed to sell other company's products, and I simply don't know**.

If you want my opinion, it's that I've never seen a product offered by a captive company that I thought would be able to compete in an open sales competition. I'm sure in narrow fact patterns it's possible for a captive product to be the "best" product for a particular consumer, but I just have never seen it.

If you think about it, it makes complete sense. If an agent is contractually obligated to sell the captive insurance company's products, where is the incentive to make the product the "best" product in the industry?

Because the captive insurance company doesn't have to compete, there simply is no financial incentive to make the products competitive (and, again, from my review of many different life insurance and annuity products, I can attest to the fact that most are not very competitive).

Much of the American economy has been built on competition. We all know that competition makes better products. Look at the auto industry. Back in the day, there used to be the Big

Three automakers in Detroit. Because they had little competition from other car makers, the Big Three got stagnant or complacent.

We went through a period of time in the auto industry where foreign competitors knew that, if they could put out a better and more reliable car, they could pick up market share. That's exactly what happened in the 1980s and 1990s. Honda, Toyota, VW, Audi, BMW, etc., started to dominate the reliability tests by Consumer Reports and others.

The American public responded by gravitating away from the Big Three.

The competition from foreign automakers pushed the Big Three to make better products; and now many of the Big Three cars are at or near the top in reliability, and companies such as Toyota are having their own reliability issues.

What's my point? That competition is good and that there is significant competition in the insurance industry among companies who are trying to gather business from "independent" advisors.

It is because of this competition that non-captive insurance companies that offer life insurance and annuity products have superior or far superior products than those offered by captive companies.

## WHAT PRODUCTS DOES THIS CHAPTER APPLY TO?

For the most part, this chapter deals with identifying "bad" insurance advisors. I'm discussing advisors who give advice on fixed life insurance or annuities (which may or may not be in the context of an overall financial or estate plan).

But the analogy of a captive agent vs. a non-captive agent also can hold true with other types of insurance. Let me list for you the different types of insurance that you can buy from a captive insurance agent or one who is independent.

-Life Insurance
    Term Life
    Whole Life
    Variable
    Universal Life
    Equity Indexed Life

(These can include group policies offered through work as well)

-Annuities

    Fixed
    Fixed Indexed

-Disability

-Auto

-Homeowners

-Business Property and Casualty

I'm going to ask you a series of questions that you can answer for yourself.

1) If you go to a Northwestern Mutual (NWM) insurance agent to buy disability or life insurance or an annuity, what company's product are they going to offer you?

Yep, you guessed it. The agent will try to sell you a NWM policy.

FYI, through my research, I've found that some NWM agents are contractually captive and some are not. The ones I've run into who are not contractually captive I've found to be mentally captive (which I'll cover shortly).

2) If you go to a State Farm agent to shop homeowners or auto insurance, what company product are you going to be offered?

Of course, you are going to be offered a State Farm product, not one offered by Progressive or Geico.

## THE BENEFIT OF WORKING WITH A TRULY INDEPENDENT AGENT

The obvious benefit of working with truly independent agents is that they are supposed to be able to shop your insurance or offer wealth-building products (life and/or annuities) from dozens, if not hundreds, of different companies.

If you read the chapter on Independent Marketing Organizations (IMOs), you know that's not always the case; but the chances of receiving better advice and being able to buy better products from an independent agent is much greater than using a captive agent.

Let's look at some obvious examples:

1) <u>Auto/homeowners</u>. Again, if you go to State Farm, you will receive a quote to buy State Farm and only State Farm insurance.

If you go to an independent agent, you should receive quotes from 2-3 different companies that the agent thinks are "best" after shopping dozens of different carriers.

The chances of finding the same coverage for less is significantly higher when using an independent agent (this is why you see State Farm and companies like Allstate airing TV commercials about how important it is to use their companies because their agents will "be there for you" when you have claims (the insinuation is that an independent agent gives inferior service or is using insurance companies that are not financially stable)).

2) <u>Cash value life insurance</u>. Maybe you read my book, <u>Retiring Without Risk</u> and have decided that you need to start allocating money to a cash value life insurance policy so you can start growing a protective tax-favorable/wealth-building tool for retirement.

If you go to a State Farm agent, you'll most likely be sold either their whole life policy or one of their variable life policies.

However, if you read my book, you'll know that, mathematically, the "best" product by far to grow wealth for retirement is an Equity Indexed Universal Life (EIUL) insurance policy.

Are you going to be offered this policy by a State Farm agent? How about a Northwestern Mutual agent? Or a Mass Mutual agent (and the list goes on and on)? The answer is no.

Why? Because the agent works for a company that either doesn't have an EIUL policy to offer clients or, what's worse, is that the company doesn't have one to offer and forbids their advisors from selling another company's products and, potentially, EIUL specifically.

If you used an independent insurance agent, the agent could offer you a number of different cash value life products including several EIUL policies from different companies.

Which type of advisor would you rather work with?

## THE DOWNSIDE TO WORKING WITH A TRULY INDEPENDENT AGENT

There is a downside to working with an independent agent. The downside is that independent agents can't offer you products from captive companies.

You are not going to have an independent agent offer you an auto or homeowner's policy from State Farm or Allstate.

You are not going to have an independent agent offer you a life insurance or annuity policy from State Farm or Northwestern Mutual.

With the advent of direct sales companies like Progressive, the chances that an independent agent will be able to offer you an auto or homeowner's policy from a direct selling company is also very low.

## EXPECTATION OF DISCLOSURE

When I have debates with Northwestern Mutual agents (a group that I frequently butt heads with), they say there is no expectation from a client that a NWM agent will bring to the table a product that is not offered by NWM.

The point being that there is no need to tell/disclose to a potential client up front that the agent is not going to shop around for the "best" products but instead is going to only bring to the table products offered by the company he/she is employed by or contractually obligated to offer.

On its face, the NWM agent has a point. Most clients who go to a NWM agent think that the agent will offer a NWM product.

What happens in the sales process is that a potential client doesn't really think much about only being offered a NWM product by a NWM agent.

Why not?

Because the agent typically will do such a great job of selling the potential client on the wonders of the company itself (it could be any captive company; I'm just using NWM as an example), the client thinks the agent is actually bringing the "best" products to the table for the client to purchase.

Let me ask you again: If you had two insurance agents in front of you and one of them could shop the "competitive" market with 5-10-15+ companies to find you the "best" products and the other was a captive agent working for one company, which one do you think you've got the "best" chance of receiving the most unbiased advice with the ultimate outcome being that you did end up with the "best" opportunity to buy the "right" or "best" products to fit your needs?

Again, to me this is a rhetorical question.

There is one last problem with the argument that the client has no expectation that a captive agent will be able to offer products from other companies. What's the problem? It's one of disclosure about the types of products the captive agent has to offer.

As stated, the company a captive agent works with may have a limited product line. While the agent may even go out of his/her way to tell the client that he/she is not able to sell products by other companies, the agent will still make the hard sell about why the captive company's products are the "best."

Even if we assume that to be the case, the product line is still limited; and, therefore, a captive agent who doesn't disclose the fact that the product line offered is limited or very limited, I would still consider to be a "bad advisor."

# MENTALLY CAPTIVE AGENTS

I'm not sure what's worse—a contractually captive agent or one who parades as an independent agent who is in reality a mentally captive agent.

What do I mean when I say mentally captive?

It's an insurance agent who has the ability to shop insurance and products with a number of different companies but chooses not to do so. The ultimate outcome of working with mentally captive agents is that you will be sold the same products from the same companies that they use for virtually all of their clients (no matter the fact pattern).

Let me go through a few obvious examples, and then I'll explain the reasons mentally captive agents exist.

**Example 1**—buying an annuity to build wealth.

Let's assume you are 55-years old and have accumulated $500,000 in an IRA for retirement. You plan on retiring in 10-15 years; and because of the recent stock market crashes and general instability of equity markets, you decide you want to build wealth with an annuity that will guarantee you a specific rate of return for as long as possible with a guaranteed income for life you can't outlive.

You sit down with your local "independent" advisor to learn about the various annuities available in the market with the expectation that the advisor will help you pick the "best" one to accomplish your goals.

Let's assume that the advisor is both securities licensed and holds a life insurance license.

Because the advisor is securities licensed, the chances of him/her knowing anything about Fixed Indexed Annuities (FIAs) is low. As you will read in the chapter on BDs and securities licensed advisors, most BDs frown on the use of FIAs and some outright forbid their licensed advisors from selling them.

Unknown to you, the advisor you are meeting with always recommends a variable annuity with an income rider at company XYZ for clients who want protection in the market and a guaranteed income for life.

What you don't know is that the advisor is not shopping the VA marketplace for the "best" VA and has never reviewed the FIAs with similar types of guaranteed riders.

To make matters worse, assume the advisor is a Certified Financial Planner (CFP®) who, in fact, does work with a BD that forbids him/her from selling FIAs.

Why worse? While I think all advisors have a fiduciary duty to provide their clients with "best" advice that is in the client's "best" interest, CFPs® tout that they have a higher fiduciary standard to follow because they are CFPs®. This is ironic since many CFPs® work through BDs that forbid them from selling FIAs and equity indexed life insurance (two tools you must be able to offer clients in order to provide them the "best" advice possible and comply with any fiduciary standard and certainly the higher standard set forth by the CFP's® board).

Getting back to the example, you give all of your financial information to the financial planner who takes it, reviews it, and sets up a meeting with you the following week to go over his "research" and provide you with his recommendation.

You meet the following week and what does the financial planner recommend to you? The same variable annuity he recommends to all his clients.

Because the financial planner took a week to come up with the recommendations and because you don't know any better, when the planner puts forth the information as to why the same variable annuity that he recommends to all of his clients is the one for you, you don't know any better and decide to sign on the dotted line to transfer your money to the VA that was recommended.

What's wrong with this picture that the client doesn't know about? A few significant things are wrong.

-The financial planner works with a BD that forbids him from selling FIAs.

-He really didn't research the VA products in the market; he really just recommended the same one he has a comfort level with and recommends to all of his clients.

What would a "good advisor" have done given the same example?

-If the advisor worked with a BD that forbids him/her from selling FIAs, this would have been disclosed so the client could find an advisor to run numbers on FIAs to compare them to the numbers offered by the VA.

-Assuming the advisor didn't have his hands tied by a BD and that he wasn't a captive insurance agent working for one insurance company, he would have done the following:

-researched all the viable FIAs in the market

-researched all the VAs in the market

-provided the data and the pros and cons of the top VA and FIA products.

If the above were done, then the client would have been receiving very good advice and then could make a full-disclosure decision as to which annuity to purchase.

As I've stated a few times in this book (sometimes with examples), the guaranteed income riders on FIAs are superior or far superior to VAs. To have literally thousands of securities licensed advisors in the industry either not know anything about FIAs or be forbidden by their BD from selling them is an outrage.

Advisors who have restrictions that are not disclosed to clients are truly the classic definition of a "bad advisor."

**Example 2**—same as above, except this time the advisor is an independent insurance agent who does NOT have a securities license.

The chances are significant that the advisor has his "go to" FIA with a guaranteed income rider. Unfortunately, that's just the way it is in the insurance industry. Few advisors want to do the research necessary to make sure that they can always offer their clients the "best" products available to fit each client's needs.

What will most likely happen is that the advisor will meet with the potential client at a second meeting (after gathering data in the first meeting) and make a recommendation to buy the same FIA with a guaranteed income rider he sells to virtually all clients.

The client thinks that by working with an independent agent that the advice given is both independent and in the client's "best" interest. Again, many times this is not the case.

What would a "good advisor" have done when helping this client?

-First the non-securities licensed advisor would have disclosed that he is not securities licensed and will not be giving the client advice on variable products or securities. Further, that there are VAs out there that have similar guaranteed income benefit riders as the FIA products that the insurance agent is going to be discussing.

The insurance agent might hand the client a copy of my **33-page white paper** detailing why FIA products with GIB riders are superior or far superior to VAs so the client can have a full-disclosure look at how both products work.

-The agent would have really shopped all the products in the marketplace to determine which one is the "best" for the client's situation.

Remember, the client said that he wanted to retire in 10-15 years. Most VA and FIA products available only roll up the guaranteed return for 10 years. However, there are a handful of products available that roll up the guaranteed rate of return (on the accumulation value) for 15-20 and some newer products that have no limit on the roll up years (although the unlimited products have lower guaranteed rates).

The question at hand is can an "independent" advisor be a "bad advisor" when it comes to offering clients the "best" annuity products? Absolutely. They can give speeches about how independent they are, but many are just as captive as contractually captive advisors because they recommend the same products over and over to clients regardless of the fact pattern and with no regard to the client's well being (if they had regard, they would shop for the "best" products to fit each clients individual situation).

### FREE TRIPS

This may or may not come as a surprise, but insurance companies often times offer free trips to advisors who place a certain amount of business with them over a specified period of time.

What kind of trips?

It depends. For X level of production, agents might earn a three-day trip to New York City where they are treated to a play on Broadway, a professional sporting event, a sightseeing tour, and, most certainly, dinner and cocktails every night at some of the best restaurants.

The agent's airfare, hotel, and other miscellaneous expenses are also taken care of. The total value of the trip might be $2,000.

If the agent qualifies for the top free trip, it could be seven days in Europe, a cruise in the Greek Islands, an Alaskan Cruise, or a trip to a beach resort in Mexico or even Jamaica. Cost of the trip can run between $5,000-$6,000.

Of course, agents are able to bring one guest with them for free.

So what? What's the big deal? Let me just tell you the big deal with an example.

Assume an agent is $10,000 in life insurance premiums short of bumping himself from the New York trip to the Greek Island Cruise trip. Assume the agent has a client coming in who can allocate $10,000 to a CVL insurance policy to grow wealth for retirement in a tax-favorable manner. Assume that the "best" policy for this client is NOT the one that will qualify the agent for the better trip. Assume that the cutoff date for new business to qualify for the trip is next week.

If the agent doesn't sell the policy from the free trip insurance company, he will be stuck going to New York for three days vs. going on the Greek Island cruise for seven days.

What does the agent do? What would you do?

I can tell you what should be done. The agent should go through a due diligence process and find the "best" products for this particular client. If it is from a company not offering this trip, that's life.

A "good advisor" always recommends products or investments that are in the "best" interest of the client. A "bad advisor" takes care of #1 first (himself/herself) even if it is at the client's expense.

Is the client going to know any better? The answer is no (unless he/she reads this book and calls me or another "good advisor" to review the situation).

Does this really happen or am I just putting forth entertaining fact patterns to make the book more interesting?

Not only does this happen, it happens on a routine basis. How do I know? Because I've talked with dozens of advisors who have admitted, without regret, that they've done this to make sure they qualify for a trip or a better trip.

### ADDITIONAL BONUSES/COMPENSATION

The free trip issue is one that is a lot less prevalent than a similar fact pattern that involves cold hard cash.

I need to discuss two different fact patterns: 1) receiving more compensation on an individual product sale; and 2) receiving a bonus (quarterly, semi-annually, or annually) for reaching certain production marks over a specified time period.

Let me discuss number one first by using an example.

It has been determined correctly that a particular client needs a fixed indexed annuity with a guaranteed income rider to meet his retirement goals of no risk and a guaranteed specific income every year for life.

There are dozens of products that agent can offer the client. However, based on the client's age and years until retirement, there are really only two products that make sense. Of the two products, one is really much better for the client (it will generate 10% more income in retirement).

However, the better product pays the agent 20% less compensation than the other suitable but not as good product.

What's the agent to do?

Assume the premium is $100,000 and the commission using the "best" product but lower compensation for the agent product is $5,000 (one-time, up-front commission). Assume the suitable but not as good product will pay the agent $7,000.

What is the agent to do?

Should he/she recommend the better product and earn $2,000 less? Absolutely. Every time this should be the answer.

Unfortunately, many times the client will be sold the inferior product so the agent can maximize his/her commission. The client will never know.

Let me move on to fact pattern number two—receiving a bonus (quarterly, semi-annually, or annually) for reaching certain production marks over a specified time period.

This is similar to the free-vacation example. Assume the agent is getting toward the end of the year. If the agent can place an additional $100,000 of annuity premiums with company X, the agent will receive a bonus on all of his/her business placed with that company for the entire year (call it a retroactive bonus).

Assume the bonus is a 1% commission on all annuity premiums and that the agent has sold $1,900,000 in annuity premiums with company X this year.

Again, the client comes in who has $100,000 that really should go into an annuity. The question is: Which annuity? After researching the products available, the agent decides again that there are two annuities that are suitable to fill the client's needs— one that is the "best" product and then one that is simply ok.

Of course, the "best" product for the client is at a company that will not help the agent qualify for the 1% bonus on what would be $2,000,000 in premiums ($20,000 bonus).

What should the agent do?

Should he recommend the better product and forego the $20,000 bonus? Absolutely. Every time this should be the answer.

Unfortunately, many times the client will be sold the inferior product so the agent can maximize commissions. The client will never know.

## RELATIONSHIP-DRIVEN SALES

The fixed life insurance and annuity business is sort of a good-old-boys club. Many relationships are formed among agents and the insurance company or independent marketing organization (IMO) at some sort of marketing event.

What kind of event? A seminar at a hotel where the agent stays free for one night at a four- or five-star hotel and then attends a half- or full-day seminar on the product line of an insurance company. An insurance company could set these up on its own; or what's more likely today is that an IMO will market it, set it up, and the insurance company will pay for it and simply show up to give the seminar.

Many times at these events the representative of the insurance company or IMO will take some of the top producing advisors out for a night on the town all expenses paid.

This gets the insurance company representative and IMO face time with the bigger producers and in a way that will make the producer think highly of the insurance company and IMO (because agents love to get free perks and free alcohol and a night on the town which is about as good as it gets for many of them).

What happens after one of these events? The agent goes back home and then the IMO and/or insurance company representative will hound the agent for premiums.

The agent will typically give some amount of premiums to the insurance company that paid for the night on the town. Why? Because for years this is how things have been done. The agent knew that he/she would have to give some business to the insurance company as payback for the freebies. Even more so, however, is that, for the agent to continue to get these freebies, the agent must send in some amount of business.

What if the insurance company that paid for the night out doesn't have very good products? That's ok; the agent doesn't have to give much business, just some business to the insurance company to keep the gravy train going. So every once in a while the agent will sell a client an inferior product (and the client will never know).

I've personally been to these dinners and nights out on the town; and I am very put off by some agents who think it is their right to be wooed by an IMO to pay for their dinner, drinks, and everything else.

Back in the day, I sold a lot of products when I had real live clients (vs. today where my clients are the advisors who I educate through my courses); and I never expected an IMO or insurance company to pick up my bill.

## SUMMARY ON MENTALLY CAPTIVE AGENTS

Again, it's tough to say which is more offensive—an agent who is contractually obligated to sell products only from the company they work for (captive agents) or ones who parade as independent advisors who act captive out of self-interest.

I find both problematic; but when it comes to mentally captive agents, I believe this is more offensive because the client has an expectation that the "best" advice is being given because the agent can shop products with multiple companies in an effort to provide clients with the "best" products.

At least with contractually captive agents, many times it is obvious that the products they are going to recommend are the ones from the insurance company they work for. Many consumers understand this (although they may not understand the consequences of using a contractually captive agent's products), and there may be no expectation of truly independent advice.

An independent, but mentally captive agent, gives the appearance of independence but may not actually be providing independent advice.

## CAREER AGENTS

Career agents are sort of a dying breed and don't fit neatly into contractually captive agents or mentally captive agents.

What is a career agent? Let me start with what is not a career agent. A non-career agent is not a W-2 employee of an insurance company. Non-career agents are NOT contractually obligated to sell ONLY the products of the employer (meaning they can sell insurance products to clients with any number of other companies).

However, career agents have **quotas they must meet** in order to continue to be a W-2 employee and receive the benefits that go along with being an employee.

Why would an agent want to be a career agent? There are a few reasons: 1) an initial salary; 2) health insurance.

When someone is just coming into the insurance business, usually they are not leaving a good job they like or leaving a profitable business they own. Most new agents who come into the insurance fields do not have a job and have very little money.

Why do you need money when becoming an insurance agent? Because it takes time to make sales and for the agent's initial commissions to come in.

If the insurance company didn't provide a reasonable salary for at least the first six-to-twelve months, most agents would leave the business before ever having a chance to succeed (they couldn't afford to be a start-up insurance salesperson).

Health insurance is the one I find more interesting. I've had a number of calls in the last year from career agents who've read my newsletters and called me to see if there was a way they could work with me in some capacity. Some want my marketing tools for free, some want me to help them with case design, some want to use me as a resource to answer tax, asset protection, or product questions, etc.

In order to work with me in any capacity that does not involve an advisor taking an educational course through The Wealth Preservation Institute (any advisor who takes my course can always contact me for questions or help), advisors must be willing to work with the IMO I work with (meaning they have to be willing to place some amount of their fixed life and/or annuity sales through the IMO I work with).

The conversation goes something like this:

<u>Agent</u>: Roccy, I've been reading your newsletters about Retirement Life™, and I'd like to learn more about it. I also noticed you have many marketing tools and that advisors you work with can get access to some of them for free. I also noticed that you help agents with finding the right products for their clients. Can you tell me more about what you do and how I can work with you?

<u>Roccy</u>: Thanks for the call. Let me ask you this question before I take the time to go over everything. Where do you currently work?

<u>Agent</u>: I'm a career agent with XYZ Company.

<u>Roccy</u>: Oh. Can you tell me if you are able to place some of your insurance sales through the IMO I work with?

<u>Agent</u>: No, I can't do that. All my products must go through the insurance company I work for.

<u>Roccy</u>: Are you able to sell fixed indexed annuities or equity indexed universal life insurance to your clients?

<u>Agent</u>: No. The company I work with doesn't offer those products, and they won't let me sell them.

<u>Roccy</u>: I don't mean to offend you, but how in the world do you give the "best" advice to your clients if you can't offer FIAs or EIUL products to them?

<u>Agent</u>: Well, that's been an issue for years; but there's nothing I can do about it.

<u>Roccy</u>: You could quit and go independent.

<u>Agent</u>: Well, I've been with the company for 20 years, and I've got really nice benefits. I also have some health issues; and if I leave the company, I won't be able to obtain or afford an individual health insurance policy.

Roccy: Again, I don't mean to offend you, but how are you able to provide your clients the "best" advice and the advice they deserve?

Agent: It's something I've thought a lot about; but, again, I'm really not in a position to go independent.

Roccy: I'm sorry to say this, but your clients deserve better.

---

Side Note—I probably have this discussion twenty times a year. Many times it's with a very nice and genuine advisor who feels really bad that he/she can't give his/her clients the "best" advice and offer the "best" products for their individual situations.

When I make the last statement, many do not get offended (some do, but most do not); they become resigned and admit to me that they know that is the case.

---

Agent: I don't disagree with you, but I'm not prepared to change what I do or the way I do it at this time.

Roccy: Let me answer your initial question about how I work with advisors. The only way I can work with advisors outside of them taking an educational course (because there are no restrictions on who can take them or the benefit that goes with taking a course) is if they are truly independent advisors.

I can't and don't work with career agents or captive agents.

Agent: Why?

Roccy: Because captive or career agents won't be able to take my recommendations for their clients and use them because many times I'll be recommending a product the agent can't sell.

Agent: I'm sorry to hear that.

Roccy: I'm sorry as well. When you make the decision to go truly independent, please feel free to give me a call back.

Agent: Unless my medical conditions change, I don't foresee that happening. I need to stay a career agent to keep my health insurance.

Roccy: I'm terribly sorry for your health conditions; but again, I think you are doing yourself and your clients a tremendous disservice by not being able to give them the "best" advice and products possible.

Agent: I appreciate your position and your time today.

Roccy: No problem. Thank you for the call.

Pretty terrifying discussion isn't it? This is real world. I really do have this exact conversation several times a year. The agent is more interested in himself than the well being of his clients.

Minimum premiums—this was not a perfect example. I used an example agent who was not allowed to sell FIAs or EIULs. Some career agents can sell FIAs and EIULs and some can't. It depends on the insurance company they work with.

What doesn't change is that a career agent has minimum production requirements in order to maintain his/her benefits. Let me start another conversation with a career agent that will crystallize this better.

I'll pick it up in the middle of the discussion:

Roccy: Are you able to sell FIAs and/or EIULs?

Agent: Yes, it's frowned upon; but we can sell them if we deem them to be the "best" products for a client.

Roccy: What company do you work for?

Agent: XYZ.

Roccy: I know that company well; most of their products are terrible.

Agent: Yes, I know.

Roccy: Why do you sell them then?

Agent: The company pays for all my medical benefits.

Roccy: So, you just said their products are terrible. What about your clients? Don't you want to offer them the "best" products?

Agent: I do for the most part. I only have to sell X amount of products with the company I work for to keep my benefits. I meet that quota every year, and then the rest of the time I sell other products I like much better.

Roccy: You're kidding me, right?

Agent: No

This is when I typically will get on my ethic high horse and give a speech about why what the agent is doing is wrong and then I wonder how he can look himself in the mirror every day knowing that some of his clients are sold inferior products just so he can meet his quota. The speech is typically ignored, and I usually will never hear from the agent again.

What's ironic is that, if career agents in the previous discussions had any decent sales each year, they would make 20-30% more money in commissions than they do being a career agent. Because of the benefits provided career agents, the commission payout on products sold is much lower than a truly independent agent.

I suppose it's easy for me to take such a hard line. I've got no current health conditions, and I can afford to pay my family's health insurance premiums.

Would I compromise myself and my clients for the sake of health insurance? I sure hope not. I hope I would seek out a different field where I could obtain health insurance through an employer where my job duties would not suffer because of my health condition (meaning my clients would not be harmed because of my inability to give them the "best" advice).

Keep in mind that I gave both agents a pretty hard time (although I try to do it in a nice, matter-a-fact way).

Many of the agents who call me, like the first one I discussed, really do want to do what's in their client's "best" interest. However, because of health insurance, they just don't want to leave the career system.

## SUMMARY ON CAPTIVE AGENTS

I know this sounds harsh, but I cannot find any redeeming qualities to contractually captive or mentally captive agents.

Contractually captive agents can't offer clients the "best" advice or products.

Mentally captive agents choose not to give their clients the "best" advice or products.

Both are equally reprehensible.

Your "best" course of action is not to work with either. The problem is how do you know or how can you tell?

## QUESTIONS TO ASK AGENTS TO DETERMINE IF THEY ARE "BAD ADVISORS"

1) Who do you work for? If the agent says he/she is a W-2 employee of an insurance company, you know he/she is a captive or career agent.

2) Are you limited in the types of products you can sell (can they sell FIAs or EIULs or variable products)? Being limited doesn't make the advisor a "bad advisor." You are just looking for the disclosure so you can make the determination to seek a second opinion on the products recommended.

3) Are you limited in the products you can offer? This is a trick question. Every agent has limits. Even independent agents have limits (they can't offer products offered by captive companies).

Even though it's a trick question, it is still a good one to ask. The agent might be able to sell FIAs but be limited to only selling products from a select few companies (many BDs who allow their reps to sell FIAs only allow them to sell a limited menu of products. Most of the time these are some of the worst products in the market).

4) Are you a career agent? The advisor could have answered that he/she is NOT captive; but as you now know, career agents who can sell other products not offered by the company they work for have quotas they have to meet. It is important to know if the agent in front of you has quotas to meet.

The good news is that these questions will help you determine if you are dealing with a captive or career agent. The bad news is that these questions will not help you determine if you are dealing with an independent but still mentally captive agent.

Hopefully, by fully reading this book and by asking some other probing questions, you'll be able to make a good assessment of your agent to determine if he/she is a "good" one or a "bad" one.

# Chapter 4
# Broker Dealers and Securities Licensed Advisors

When I discuss why I think Broker Dealers (BDs) can be bad for the financial services industry, securities licensed advisors cringe. After reading this chapter, you'll understand why.

What you won't understand is why securities licensed advisors go along with the mandates of BDs which, many times, are to the detriment of their clients.

Like many of the other chapters of this book, by the end of this chapter, your blood may be at a boil (and I wouldn't blame you).

## DEFINITIONS

### What is a Broker Dealer (BD)?

A BD is a company that is in the business of buying and selling securities.

### What is a security?

Stocks and mutual funds are the classic examples of securities that most people will be familiar with.

BDs must register with the Securities and Exchange Commission (SEC) as well as FINRA (Financial Industry Regulatory Authority).

### What is a stock broker?

A general definition is an individual who sells securities to the general consumer (the "client").

In order for stock brokers to sell a stock, mutual fund, or other type of security, they need a securities license. The following are the most common types of licenses and what it allows an advisor to sell to clients.

-**Series 6 License**—this license allows advisors to sell a limited menu of securities such as mutual funds, variable life insurance, and variable annuities.

-**Series 7**—this license allows advisors to sell individual stocks, bonds, options, etc. In order to conduct business, an advisor must also obtain either a Series 63 or 66.

-**Series 63**—this license is required by each state and authorizes licensees to transact business within the state.

-**Series 65**—this is a fee-only license. You can think of a Series 65 as an equivalent license to a Series 7 except that with a Series 65 the advisor cannot earn "commissions."

-**Series 66**—this license is simply the name of one that combines both the Series 63 and 65.

## COMMISSIONS AND FEES

These are just what you'd think they are. If an advisor sells a mutual fund that is "loaded" correctly, the advisor can make an up-front commission on its sale to clients. This is in addition to a money-management fee generated and paid to the securities licensed advisor typically on an annual basis.

Here are some typical commissions that can be generated by securities licensed advisors when they sell certain products:

-Sales Charge (Load) on Purchases—this is a fee that investors pay when buying an investment that reduces the amount available to invest. For example, if an investor writes a $10,000 check to a fund for the purchase of fund shares and the fund has a 5% front-end sales load, the total amount of the sales load will be $500.

The $500 sales load is first deducted from the $10,000 check (and typically paid to a selling broker); and assuming no other front-end fees, the remaining $9,500 is used to purchase fund shares for the investor.

-Deferred Sales Charge (Load)—this is a fee that investors pay when they redeem fund shares (that is, sell their shares back to the fund) (also known as "back-end" sales load). No sales load is deducted at purchase (meaning all of the investor's money is immediately used to purchase fund shares) (assuming that no other fees or charges apply at the time of purchase).

If there is a deferred load of 5%, it is not deducted until the investor redeems his or her shares. Usually this load is based on the *lesser* of the value of the shareholder's initial investment or the value of the shareholder's investment at redemption.

The most common type of back-end sales load is the "Contingent Deferred Sales Load," also referred to as a "CDSC," or "CDSL." The amount of this type of load will depend on how long the investor holds his or her shares and typically decreases to zero if the investor holds his or her shares long enough.

For example, a CDSL might be 5% if an investor holds his or her shares for one year, 4% if the investor holds his or her shares for two years, and so on until the load goes away completely. The rate at which this fee will decline will be disclosed in the fund's prospectus.

A fund or class with a CDSL typically will also have an annual 12b-1 fee.

-12b-1 Fee—this is a fee paid by a fund out of fund assets to cover distribution expenses and sometimes shareholder service expenses. "12b-1 fees" get their name from the SEC rule that authorizes a fund to pay them. The rule permits a fund to pay distribution fees out of fund assets only if the fund has adopted a plan (12b-1 plan) authorizing their payment.

"Distribution fees" include fees paid for marketing and selling fund shares, such as compensating brokers and others who sell fund shares, paying for advertising, the printing and mailing of prospectuses to new investors, and the printing and mailing of sales literature.

The SEC does not limit the size of 12b-1 fees that funds may pay. But under FINRA rules, 12b-1 fees that are used to pay marketing and distribution expenses (as opposed to shareholder service expenses) cannot exceed 0.75 percent of a fund's average net assets per year.

Some 12b-1 plans also authorize and include "shareholder service fees," which are fees paid to persons to respond to investor inquiries and provide investors with information about their investments.

A fund may pay shareholder service fees without adopting a 12b-1 plan. If shareholder service fees are paid outside a 12b-1 plan, then they will be included in the "Other Expenses" category. FINRA imposes an annual .25% cap on shareholder service fees (regardless of whether these fees are authorized as part of a 12b-1 plan).

-Other Expenses—included in this category are expenses not included in the categories "Management Fees" or "Distribution and/or Service (12b-1) Fees." Examples include: shareholder service expenses that are not included in the "Distribution and/or Service (12b-1) Fees" category; custodial expenses; legal expenses; accounting expenses; transfer agent expenses; and other administrative expenses.

**What about No-Load Funds?**

With all this talk about fees on "loaded" mutual funds, I'm sure that many of you are thinking that it is best to use "no-load" funds.

Some funds call themselves "no-load." As the name implies, this means that the fund does not charge any type of sales load. Not every type of shareholder fee is a "sales load," and a no-load fund may charge fees that are not sales loads.

For example, a no-load fund is permitted to charge purchase fees, redemption fees, exchange fees, and account fees, none of which is considered to be a "sales load." In addition, under FINRA rules, a fund is permitted to pay its annual operating expenses and still call itself "no-load" unless the combined amount of the fund's 12b-1 fees or separate shareholder service fees exceeds 0.25% of the fund's average annual net assets.

-Redemption Fee—a redemption fee is another type of fee that some funds charge their shareholders when the shareholders redeem their shares. Although a redemption fee is deducted from redemption proceeds just like a deferred sales load, it is not considered to be a sales load. Unlike a sales load, which is used to pay brokers, a redemption fee is typically used to defray fund costs associated with a shareholder's redemption and is paid directly to the fund, not to a broker.

The SEC limits redemption fees to 2%. The SEC has adopted a rule addressing the imposition of redemption fees by mutual funds in Rule 22c-2 of the Investment Company Act of 1940.

-Exchange Fee—an exchange fee is a fee that some funds impose on shareholders if they exchange (transfer) to another fund within the same fund group.

-Account Fee—an account fee is a fee that some funds separately impose on investors in connection with the maintenance of their accounts. For example, some funds impose an account maintenance fee on accounts whose value is less than a certain dollar amount.

-Purchase Fee—a purchase fee is another type of fee that some funds charge their shareholders when the shareholders purchase their shares. A purchase fee differs from, and is not considered to be, a front-end sales load because a purchase fee is paid to the fund (not to a broker) and is typically imposed to defray some of the fund's costs associated with the purchase.

**More Fees—**

Don't forget about the fees that can and usually are added on to either a loaded or no-load mutual fund.

-Management Fees—management fees are fees that are paid out of fund assets to the fund's investment advisor (or its affiliates) for managing the fund's investment portfolio and administrative fees payable to the investment advisor (small accounts usually pay a 1% annual fee for management services. The percentage typically decreases with the size of the account).

-Total Annual Fund Operating Expenses—this fee is the total of a fund's annual fund operating expenses expressed as a percentage of the fund's average net assets (like a 1.2% annual expense that is on top any other expense).

Fees are not an issue in the absence of value!

The title to this paragraph is one of my favorite quotes of all time. If you are receiving equal value for the fees you pay, then you should not have a problem paying them. However, most of the time investors have no idea what the fees are, whether they are worth paying, and certainly do not understand how they affect how money grows.

A "good advisor" will go out of his/her way to detail every fee you are paying to invest money with him/her. A "bad advisor" will not.

## NAMES OF SEVERAL BDs YOU MIGHT BE FAMILIAR WITH

Have you heard of LPL Financial, Merrill Lynch, A.G. Edwards, Raymond James Financial Services, Inc., AXA Advisors LLC, Northwestern Mutual, or Waterstone Financial Group?

## WHAT DOES A BD DO?

Depending on whom you ask, you'll get different answers. If you ask me, most BDs do very little except prevent securities licensed advisors from providing their clients the "best" unbiased advice possible and from telling their clients the whole truth.

Technically speaking, however, in addition to being the clearing company that allows stock brokers to sell stocks, mutual funds, etc., a BD is supposed to function in an oversight capacity.

What do I mean when I say oversight? I mean the BD is supposed to make sure that the advisors it licenses are "doing the right thing" for their clients (this is ironic since in my opinion many BDs do just the opposite).

BDs are supposed to provide training to advisors on how to conduct business properly and are supposed to act as the big brother in the sky that oversees/watches what its licensed advisors are doing.

Many BDs bring significant resources to the table to help their licensed advisors with research on stocks, mutual funds, bonds, etc. Many BDs have their own sometimes sizable in-house research teams who conduct their own research and make recommendations to licensed brokers who are positioned all over the country.

If you think the majority of stock brokers actually do their own research before recommending the purchase of stocks, mutual funds, and bonds, you are dreaming.

Do you really think your "local" broker has time to research all the stocks, mutual funds, bonds, etc., in each sector (growth, value, income, small cap, large cap, etc.)? They don't have the time, and the vast majority do not have the expertise to do so.

Therefore, when most stock brokers recommend to a client a particular type of investment, many times that investment recommendation came down from the research department at the BD.

The previous list of functions that a BD does is a brief list. BDs have many duties and do a whole host of things that for this book are totally unimportant (which is why I've not listed much in this book).

## BD LIABLITY

BDs are liable for the acts of their licensed advisors. Therefore, if their advisors sell clients "unsuitable" investments that cause clients harm, when the lawsuits come down, the BD is ultimately liable.

The BD might not have done anything wrong (meaning that no oversight could have prevented the harm), but, yet, the BD is still liable.

Because of this ultimate liability and the fact that lawsuits against securities licensed advisors spiked significantly after the last stock market crash (-59% from the highs of 2007 to the lows of 2008), do you think that BDs are giving more or less oversight to their advisors? The answer is not only more oversight but much more oversight. Oversight comes from a BD's compliance department.

## BD COMPLIANCE

To most securities licensed advisors, the word compliance is a four-letter word.

Most securities licensed advisors see their BD like a communist dictator who tells them what to do and who watches every move they make.

85

Monitoring of communications—did you know that "all" communications between a securities licensed advisor who works with a BD must be reviewed (or have the ability to be reviewed) by the BD?

That's right. Every e-mail that is sent to a client or potential client is saved on the BD's server for review. You might think that this is not a big deal because no BD could possibly read all the e-mails; and so what if they do, right?

LPL Financial, one of the largest BDs, has 285 compliance professionals.

Understand that I send out educational e-newsletters to over 300,000 licensed advisors every week. I can't tell you the number of advisors who have requested that I use their "personal" e-mail instead of their business e-mail. Why? So big brother (BD compliance) doesn't see my newsletters and so the advisor can communicate with me without oversight from the compliance department.

Every letter that is sent to a client has to be kept in the event of a BD audit (where the BD compliance department actually sends someone out to an advisor's office to conduct a compliance audit).

All marketing material must be approved by compliance before it makes it to clients or potential clients.

If this sounds insane, it gets much worse. As you will read, many BDs limit the ability of an advisor to deal with certain topics. I find this one of the biggest outrages in our industry and part of the book that I believe readers will be most offended by.

On the bright side, not every advisor who sells securities has to work directly with a broker dealer.

## SELLING THROUGH A BD

If advisors have a Series 7 license, they must sell their securities through a BD. Registered Investment Advisors (RIAs) do not have to sell securities through a BD as long as they have a Series 65 and 63 license or a Series 66 license that is the combo of 65 and 63.

## WHAT IS A REGISTERED INVESTMENT ADVISOR (RIA)?

An RIA is a licensed professional that registers with the Securities and Exchange Commission (SEC) and any states in which he or she operates. Most RIAs are partnerships or corporations but individuals can also register as RIAs.

RIAs give investment advice to clients but are paid much like mutual fund managers. RIAs usually earn their revenue through a management fee comprised of a percentage of assets held for a client. RIAs **do not make money from securities commissions** like a typical advisor selling/clearing sales through a BD.

Fees fluctuate, but the average is around 1%. Generally, the more assets a client has, the lower the fee he or she can negotiate - sometimes as little as 0.35%. This serves to align the best interests of the client with those of the RIA as the advisor cannot make any more money on the account unless the client increases his or her asset base (vs. a transactional salesperson who makes money on the sale of securities (the more turnover a portfolio has, the more money a commission-based advisor can make)).

As a general statement, RIAs typically cater to a high-net-worth investor (someone with a net worth of $1 million or more). The reason for this is that most RIA firms will establish an account minimum for anyone wishing to become a client. Amounts below this tend to be more difficult to manage while still making a profit.

An RIA can create portfolios using individual stocks, bonds, and mutual funds. RIA firms can cover the spectrum as far as what goes into their clients' portfolios. They may use a mix of funds and individual issues or only funds as a way to streamline asset allocation and cut down on commission costs.

In short, RIAs do not make money from commissions when securities are sold. Instead, they charge asset-based fees which seem to align their interest more with the long-term success of a client vs. short-term success based on an actively traded portfolio with high turnover in stocks/mutual funds (which means high commission sales for non-RIA advisors).

## RIA COMPLIANCE/OVERSIGHT

Unlike non-RIAs who have to deal with the nightmare of a BD compliance department, RIAs only have to worry about the state regulators and the Securities and Exchange Commission (SEC).

That means an RIA does not have to get approval for advertising material and doesn't have big brother reading all of their e-mails. That means an RIA does not have his/her hands tied when it comes to deciding what products or wealth-building/retirement tools are best for clients.

## PROTECTING THE BD, NOT THE CLIENT

It is my opinion that many BDs are more interested in protecting themselves from lawsuits than helping their licensed advisors provide the best advice to their clients.

How do many BDs protect themselves from lawsuits? They limit the type of advice and products that can be sold to clients.

Think about that for a minute. Would you want to work with an advisor who is forbidden from giving certain financial advice or offering certain financial or insurance products even if the advice or financial instrument is in your "best" interest?

Or would you rather work with an advisor who does not have limits on the type of advice he/she can give to you and can bring to the table all of the viable financial instruments or products for you to use to protect and grow your wealth?

The previous questions are really rhetorical because everyone will answer them the same way (that it is always better to work with an advisor who does not have restrictions on the advice given or the financial instruments or products available).

Why do BDs limit the advice an advisor can give or the products they can sell? Again, the answer is simple. BDs are looking to avoid lawsuits.

## WHAT TYPE OF ADVICE AND PRODUCTS ARE OFF LIMITS?

It will depend on the BD. Each one has its own list of areas of advice and products that the BD does not want an advisor to discuss or sell. However, the following is a brief list of the ones I find the most offensive.

-Life Settlements—what is a life settlement (LS)? It's when a person who owns a life insurance policy no longer needs or wants the policy and decides to sell it for cash.

Why would someone sell a life insurance policy?

1) When the policy owner has insurance and/or estate needs that have changed, which makes their current policy(s) inadequate or excessive for their current or future needs.

-Estate size shrunk

-Beneficiary predeceased

-Pay off a loan that no longer exists

2) When premiums on the policy are no longer affordable.

3) When a policy owner is not satisfied with the performance of the insurance product(s) they have chosen or are aware of newer, better performing insurance products. If the owner can get more from an LS than surrender, it makes sense to sell vs. surrender.

4) When a policy owner chooses to realize the value of their policy(s) now rather than continuing to pay on a policy from which they will never receive benefits. Policy owners decide that they no longer want to fund the policy and want to reap any benefits from the policy today.

5) When a policy owner wishes to live out the remaining years of life without a change in lifestyle.

This is the classic situation where someone has been paying on a policy for 20+ years and is now in retirement. He/she may or may not have an estate tax problem but has had a lifestyle change.

The policy owner may not have enough money to live the accustomed lifestyle until the presumed date of death. Therefore, selling a policy for cash now may be financially prudent.

6) When a policy owner can't afford the policy and needs capital to pay for medical treatments or procedures.

I'm not trying to make readers experts in life settlements. My point is simply to point out that they can be an important financial tool for clients 65-years old or older.

Do you think that a "financial planner" with a securities license should be able to talk with their clients about the proper use of life settlements in an overall financial/estate plan?

My opinion, and I'm guessing that 99.9% of those who read this book will agree, is that the answer is a resounding yes.

Why don't some BDs allow their clients to give advice on or help broker sales of life insurance policies? Liability. There have been a number of lawsuits in the life settlement industry, and BDs simply do not want to run the risk that their advisor might do something wrong and expose themselves and the BD to lawsuits.

Is the intentional avoidance of a useful retirement/financial planning/estate planning concept such as life settlements good for the consumer? NO!

Is an advisor who has his/her hands tied by a BD when dealing with life settlements a "bad advisor?" Maybe. If the advisor knows that a life settlement is a viable option for a client and doesn't disclose to the client that it is a potential solution that the advisor cannot help with (and then suggest that the client find an advisor who can help), then I would consider the advisor a "bad advisor."

-Reverse Mortgages (RM)—a reverse mortgage is a special and different kind of loan that is easy to obtain if you are at least 62-years of age and own your own home, condo (PUD), or co-op (only in New York). There is no credit or financial underwriting with an RM. You simply need a house with equity (which means it is very easy to qualify for).

A reverse mortgage converts a portion of the value (equity) of a home into instant cash. The pool of money that is created by a reverse mortgage can be received by a senior homeowner(s) in a variety of ways.

RMs are non-recourse loans. The only collateral for the loan is the home.

RMs require no servicing (meaning there are no monthly payments). An RM loan is typically paid back at the death of a client from the proceeds of the sale of the home by the heirs.

Why would someone 62-years and older want to use an RM?

Keep in mind that many people have not done well saving money over the last 10-20+ years. However, the one thing they have done diligently is pay their mortgage. Therefore, there are a lot of broke people out there who have no cash and paid-off homes.

1) To pay medical bills. As I just stated, there are many people who don't have much money but who have paid-off homes. If they have medical bills they can't pay or life sustaining or improving drugs that are expensive, an RM might be a way to help pay for these expenses.

2) Reduce estate taxes. This is one that advisors who tout themselves as financial planners or knowledgeable on estate planning should know.

There are hundreds of thousands of Americans who have estates worth in excess of $2,000,000 and even $5,000,000. One of the most difficult assets to deal with in an estate plan is the personal residence. Affluent clients do not want and do not need to sell their homes before they die. Many of these homes are worth $500,000 or more.

If someone with an estate tax problem dies with a $500,000 home inside the estate, estate taxes of 40% will be levied on the asset (federal estate tax rate) at death. Therefore, the house is not worth $500,000 to the heirs; it's really worth $300,000 after taxes.

A good financial/estate planning tool to mitigate this issue is the use of an RM. For example, if the homeowner takes out a $200,000 RM, gifts that to an irrevocable life insurance trust, a life insurance policy with let's say a $650,000+ death benefit can be purchased. That death benefit is outside of the estate and will pass to the heirs free of estate taxes.

The homeowner is able to leverage an asset that is only worth 45 cents on the dollar to significantly increase the size of the after-tax estate for his/her heirs.

I'm not trying to make readers experts in RMs. My point is simply to point out that they can be an important financial tool for clients 62-years or older.

Do you think that a "financial planner" with a securities license should be able to talk with their clients about the proper use of RMs in an overall financial/estate plan?

My opinion, and I'm guessing that 99.9% of those who read this book will agree, is that the answer is a resounding yes.

Why don't some BDs allow their clients to give advice on or help broker sales of RMs? Liability. There have been a number of lawsuits in the RM industry, and BDs simply do not want to run the risk that their advisors might do something wrong and expose themselves and the BD to lawsuits.

Is the intentional avoidance of a useful retirement/financial planning/estate planning concept such as RMs good for the consumer? NO!

Is an advisor who has his/her hands tied by a BD when dealing with RMs a "bad advisor?" Maybe. If the advisor knows that an RM is a viable option for a client and doesn't disclose to the client that it is a potential solution that the advisor cannot help with (and then suggest that the client find an advisor who can help), then I would consider the advisor a "bad advisor."

### FIXED INDEXED ANNUITIES (FIAs)

Do you know what an FIA is? Chances are that, if you are only receiving advice from a securities licensed advisor, the answer is no.

One of the main motivating factors that drove me to write this book will be covered in the next several pages. I was so disgusted with the securities industry and how it deals with FIAs that I decided to write this book (no kidding).

What is an FIA? It is a tax-deferred annuity with the following features:

1) Money **NEVER goes backwards** when the stock market goes negative.

2) Growth in an FIA grows with the stock market up to a cap. Not all products have caps, but most of them do. Annual caps range from a low of 4% in low interest rate environments to in excess of 12% in higher interest rate environments.

3) **Gains are locked in annually** and can **never be lost**.

4) Many products have guaranteed income riders that will **guarantee a rate of return** on an accumulation value (not walk-away value) in the accumulation phase coupled with a **guaranteed income for life** that can't be outlived.

5) Some products have a free, long-term care benefit.

A visual for an FIA in the growth phase (one without a guaranteed income rider) would look like the following:

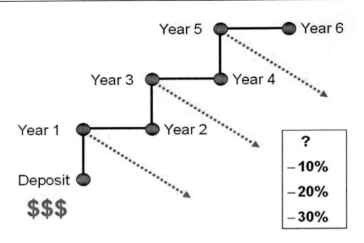

### ZERO IS YOUR HERO

A good saying when the market goes negative is that "zero is your hero." It's a saying that people who had FIAs during the 2000-2002 and 2007-2008 stock market crashes started to use.

Instead of going over to your neighbor's house and bragging about how well your stocks did in a bull market (which many people have a tendency to do), you would go over there and brag about how you earned ZERO. It's crazy; but in the volatile environment we are in, when the stock market goes negative (or very negative) in a short period of time, zero sure is your hero.

Let's look at an example of zero being your hero over a five-year period with returns of 14.71%, **-22%**, **-11%**, **-9%**, and 21% where the starting account value is $100,000.

| | $100,000 | $100,000 |
|---|---|---|
| | Invested in S&P | Invested in FIA |
| Year | A | B |
| 1 | $114,710 | $112,000 |
| 2 | $89,370.56 | $112,000 |
| 3 | $78,753.34 | $112,000 |
| 4 | $71,586.78 | $112,000 |
| 5 | $86,648.64 | $122,080 |

As you can see, when the stock market goes backwards, so does the account balance invested in the S&P 500 stock index. However, in those same negative years, the FIA flat lined and held its highest value which came at end of year one.

Also, you'll notice that, in the first positive year, the account value in the S&P 500 stock index was higher than the FIA account balance. That's because most FIAs have caps on the upside growth; and, in this particular example, the cap in year one was 12%.

FIAs are not the perfect wealth-building tool. However, based on their protective design, it is easy for millions of Americans (especially those over 50-years old) to justify having some portion of their retirement money allocated to these products.

If you only knew what the stock market was going to do, wouldn't you have had some or even a significant amount of your money in a principally guaranteed FIA over the last ten years?

## GUARANTEED INCOME RIDERS

As I stated in an earlier bullet point, one of the unique benefits some FIAs have is a guaranteed rate of return on an accumulation value (not a walk-away value) coupled with a guaranteed income for life.

What if there were products out there that could guarantee you a 7-8% rate of return for 10-20 years coupled with a lifetime income you could never outlive. Would you want to know about such a product?

Let's look at an example of an FIA that is currently in the market at the time this book was printed.

Features: 8% guaranteed for up to 20 years with a payment of 6% guaranteed for life starting at age 70 (depending on when you turn on the income, the guaranteed income percentage would be higher or lower than this example. It will depend on your age at the time you turn on the income stream).

Let's look at an example. Assume the example client is 50 years old and has $500,000 in an IRA or qualified retirement plan. At age 70, the guaranteed accumulated account value that will be used for income calculation purposes would be **$2,563,526** (this product has a 10% up-front bonus that helps supercharge the accumulation value).

The $2,563,526 amount is not a walk-away amount. That amount would be approximately $1,300,000 if the actual return in the product is 5%.

If the example client turned on the income stream at age 70, the guaranteed income every year for the rest of his/her life would be **$153,812**. If the client lives until age 95+, it will keep paying.

To compare—if the $500,000 grew in a "properly balanced mix of stocks, mutual funds, and bonds" (classic advice from a securities licensed advisor) that netted a 5% return (after expenses and taxes), you would only be able to take out $153,812 every year from ages 70-81. At age 82, you would **run out of money**.

Let me ask you again—if there were a product out there that could guarantee you a 7%-8% guaranteed return (on an accumulation value) coupled with a guaranteed income for life you could never outlive, would you want to know about it? Of course you would.

Unfortunately, if you receive advice from a "bad advisor," you will not be told anything about the previously discussed FIA products.

## MANY BDs FORBID THEIR ADVISORS FROM SELLING OR EVEN DISCUSSING FIAs WITH CLIENTS

As I've stated several times, many BDs are NOT about putting the client first. Most of them are about 1) gathering assets under management, and 2) avoiding lawsuits.

Would it outrage you to know that certain BDs have formal policies that FORBID their advisors from selling FIAs? It should.

The policy will vary from BD to BD, but the policy is basically that their advisors can't discuss or sell FIAs to clients.

Which BDs don't allow their advisors to sell FIAs? Here are a few (there are many others that are not listed below):

-Mass Mutual

-Northwestern Mutual

-State Farm

-Met Life

-New York Life

Look at the following quote from a Mass Mutual agent when I asked him if he could sell FIAs to clients.

"To answer your question, we are licensed to sell FIAs but we are **not allowed to sell them** under our agent's contract. Mass does not have an FIA in its product line, and we would be **terminated if we sell the product**. Even our outside brokerage operation will **not allow us to sell any indexed products**. Hope this helps."

If the above quote doesn't send chills up your spine, I don't know what will. The advisor is confirming that, if he sells an FIA product or any indexed product (including equity indexed life insurance which you will read about in a few pages), he would be terminated from his contract with Mass Mutual.

## LACK OF DISCLOSURE IS WORSE THAN NOT BEING ABLE TO SELL FIAs

If you are not sufficiently outraged at what you've read so far, I want to discuss disclosure as an issue that I find to be even more outrageous.

Sometimes reasonable minds differ as to what are the best products/tools that should be used to help clients of various ages in different financial situations.

Is it plausible that a BD that has hundreds if not thousands of advisors giving financial planning/retirement planning advice could fully research the value of FIAs and decide that they are "all" bad products and are not ones that should be introduced to clients? I suppose so, although, from a mathematical standpoint, it would be nearly impossible to come to such a conclusion.

Be that as it may, assume that a BD research department came to this conclusion; and because of it, the compliance department decided to come down with a rule stating that no advisor licensed with the BD can sell FIAs.

One question that comes to mind is: Would a "good advisor" still take the time to research FIAs to determine if they are a product with any redeeming value for client? The answer is yes. Only "bad advisors" take the word of their BD when it comes to research on products that could potentially be good for clients.

The most important question that needs to be asked and answered is whether or not an advisor who is forbidden from selling FIAs should disclose to a client that such products exist and further disclose that the advisor can't sell such products to the client because of the rules set forth by the BD.

The answer to this question is quite simple. For ANY advisor touting himself/herself as a financial planner or retirement planner (this includes anyone who is a CFP®), the answer is YES!

How can a financial planner who sells himself/herself to clients as someone with unique skills not disclose to a client that he/she can't sell a product that never has losses, locks gains in annually (up to a cap), can come with a free long-term care rider, can guarantee a return on an accumulation value of between 7-8%

that is coupled with a guaranteed income for life that a client can never outlive?

How could an advisor look himself/herself in the face knowing that these products are out there; and, just because they made the mistake of hanging their securities license with the wrong BD, they can't sell such products or even discuss them with clients?

You want to know how most advisors look themselves in the face in spite of what you've read?

It's really simple—a high percentage of securities licensed advisors don't even know what an FIA is, how it works, and that the guaranteed income riders on FIAs are better or far better than the ones they are selling in the variable annuity products they offer.

If you think I'm kidding, I'm not. If I had a dollar for every securities licensed advisor I've talked with over the last five years who told me they didn't know anything about FIAs, I'd be able to take several months off and vacation in the islands somewhere.

Why don't most securities licensed advisors know anything or very little about FIAs? You probably guessed it by now. The answer is because most look to their BD for education and product recommendations. If their BD forbids them from selling FIAs, they certainly are not receiving education about them.

I could respect to a point a securities licensed advisor who discloses to a client up front that he/she can't talk about or sell FIAs and that the client might want to seek advice elsewhere before making a decision as to where to position money to grow wealth for retirement. I've never heard of an advisor making that disclosure; but if I did, I would not consider the advisor to be a "bad advisor."

## WHY DON'T MOST BDs LIKE FIAs?

I've no official response to my inquiries on this question. I can tell you what the obvious practical answer is. BDs make most of their money when an advisor gathers millions of dollars under management. BDs make money every year when an advisor manages an actively traded portfolio through the BD.

FIAs typically pay a one-time, up-front commission. The amount of money a BD can make on that one-time commission is not very large. Can you imagine with the two stock market crashes we've had in the last several years what would happen if clients who had their money with a securities licensed advisor found out about the power and protective nature of FIAs?

How many clients age 50 and older would demand that their securities licensed advisor move money to an FIA that guarantees a 7-8% rate of return coupled with a lifetime income that can't be outlived (in a product with no stock market risk)? Most of the clients would request that some or even a large portion of their money be moved into FIAs.

What would that do to the profitability of the BD? It would decrease dramatically.

### VARIABLE ANNUITIES (VAs)

I wanted to touch briefly on VAs. Most advisors who sell stocks/mutual funds and bonds through a BD can sell clients VAs.

What is a VA? It's a tax-deferred annuity where money is allowed to grow tax-deferred (without capital gains or dividend taxes).

How does a VA differ from an FIA? VAs have a much higher upside on the money invested (basically unlimited). FIAs typically have caps on the gains annually. VAs have no floor (meaning, if the stock market tanks, so does the account value in a VA). FIAs never lose money and lock in gains annually. VAs have very high internal fees (sometimes up to 4% if you add on all the riders). FIAs typically have no fees (however, they do have caps on the gains).

VAs also have a number of riders. The one that's important for this chapter is the guaranteed income rider. That's right. VAs have the same kind of rider I just discussed and touted as a wonderful option with FIAs.

If that's the case, then what's the big deal about securities licensed advisors not being allowed to sell FIAs? It's a big deal because the riders on FIA products are either superior or far superior to those offered in VAs.

## WHAT IS A "BAD ADVISOR?"

A "bad advisor" is one who sells securities through a BD that forbids them from selling FIAs.

If an advisor works with such a BD and discloses the fact that he/she is not allowed to sell such products but goes on to tell clients that they are products the client might want to look at before making a decision about what to do with their money, this would not be considered a "bad advisor."

## NOT ALL SECURITIES ADVISORS HAVE THEIR HANDS TIED

Even though I just spent the last several pages telling you my distain for BDs and how they tie the hands of the advisors who sell through the BDs, there are a few BDs that "get it."

There are some BDs who allow their licensed advisors to discuss and sell FIAs and equity indexed life insurance (discussed in the next section of this book). The BDs who allow this don't usually encourage it, but it is nice to know that some securities licensed advisors can provide advice to clients on what I believe are two of the best and most protective wealth-building tools clients have at their disposal.

I can nearly guarantee you this—if a securities licensed advisor gives you my book to read, the chance that his/her BD allows him/her to discuss and recommend the protective wealth-building tools in this book is significant.

## EQUITY INDEXED UNIVERSAL LIFE (EIUL) INSURANCE

One of my favorite wealth-building tools for clients under the age of 55 is a properly designed and funded EIUL policy.

Like some, I believe that Cash Value Life (CVL) insurance is considered an asset class. People build wealth through stocks, bonds, real estate, etc., and many should grow wealth through cash value life insurance.

I'll try to be brief in this book when it comes to explaining why CVL insurance can be such a tremendous wealth-building tool. However, if you would like to know much more about how you can use CVL to grow your wealth in a protected and tax-favorable manner, go to www.retiringwithoutrisk.com. There you will be able to learn more and even buy a copy of my book Retiring Without Risk (a book 50% devoted to building wealth with CVL and 50% devoted to using FIAs as unique, protective, and powerful retirement tools).

### WHY BUILD WEALTH WITH CVL INSURANCE?

Tell me if you would like to use a wealth-building tool with the following attributes:

1) Money grows tax-free.

2) Money can be removed tax-free.

3) Money grows at market rates (with caps that range from 10-15% annually).

4) Money does not go backwards due to stock market losses.

5) Gains are locked-in annually

6) It is a tool that will self-complete its funding when you die (meaning that, if you only funded it one year and then died, it would fully fund as though you had funded it every year until retirement).

7) Some EIUL policies provide a free long-term care benefit.

8) One EIUL policy comes with a guaranteed income benefit rider.

If you're asking yourself if I'm really talking about cash value life insurance, the answer is yes. Certain CVL insurance policies have all of the above-mentioned attributes.

Again, I'm not going to get into the math behind CVL insurance; but a properly designed policy can generate more or significantly more after-tax cash in retirement than investing in a brokerage account, a tax-deferred qualified plan (or IRA), or even a Roth IRA or Roth 401(k).

The point of this part of the chapter isn't to prove that the previously mentioned positive attributes actually exist. The point is to help you determine if you are using a "good" or "bad" advisor. That will be determined by whether an advisor knows about the type of policy I'm discussing and whether he/she is allowed to sell it.

### TYPES OF LIFE INSURANCE POLICIES

There are several different types of life insurance policies.

There are what I call old-school/very-conservative policies known as <u>whole life</u>. These policies are not going to make you rich, but they are nice steady tax-favorable/wealth-building tools. I don't typically recommend whole life for wealth-building unless the client is ultra-conservative and understands the limited growth potential.

There are <u>universal life</u> policies. These, too, are conservative policies similar to whole life in that policy owners won't get rich using one but also won't have to worry about stock market crashes, etc. These policies should return modest rates of return (2% more than CD/money market rates over time). I don't recommend universal life policies very often unless it's in the context of estate planning. Then I recommend a unique type of policy that is designed for the maximum guaranteed death benefit, not one designed to grow cash in a tax-favorable manner for retirement.

Then there are <u>Variable Universal Life</u> insurance (VUL) policies. This is the policy of choice by most securities licensed advisors when using one to help a client grow money in a tax-favorable manner for retirement. These are the types of policies BDs like to see their advisors sell. Why? Because it fits with the BD business model of making annual fees on money under management.

VUL policies are fairly simple to explain. You pay your life insurance premium to the company where the insurance costs are the lowest possible current year's term insurance cost for an owner based on his/her age (which is great when you are young and very expensive when you are older). The money not allocated to the costs in the policy is invested at the policyholder's direction, which is typically into mutual funds.

Because of the unique nature of all properly designed life insurance policies, money in the VUL can grow tax-free and be removed tax-free in retirement. Sounds great, right? It actually is great as long as the market goes up.

Policy owners have an unlimited ability to earn money in a VUL. If the mutual funds earn returns of 10-20-30+%, that return is credited on the cash in the policy. There are no capital gains or dividend taxes due; and, again, the money can be removed tax-free in retirement (or before if needed).

If you can't tell, I'm leading up to what I don't like about VULs. What don't I like about them? They have an unlimited floor. Meaning, if the stock market tanks -20-30-40-50% (like it has recently), the cash invested in your life insurance policy goes down with it (and you also have the insurance costs and money management fees on top of the losses in the policy each year).

Because of other types of policies in the market, there is really no need for a VUL policy except for those people who think over time the stock market is going to go on another bull run.

What if there were a CVL policy that could earn returns of 15% a year with NO risk of loss? What if the same policy locked in the investment gains every year never to be lost due to a stock market crash? What if the policy also had a guaranteed income rider that could guarantee an income for life that a client could never outlive?

Another way to get at my point would be to ask the following question:

Would you rather have a policy that had an unlimited upside and an unlimited floor where the gains could be hit with losses of 50% or more in a short period of time?

Or would you rather have a policy that limits the upside in the policy to 13-15% a year but where the gains are locked-in annually, the money in the policy can never go backwards due to stock market losses, and when you are ready to turn on an income stream from the policy in retirement, the policy has a guaranteed income rider that will pay you a guaranteed payment each year that you can never outlive?

For most, a policy with good upside potential and no ability to lose money due to stock market losses is going to be the policy of choice.

What policy am I describing? An **Equity Indexed Universal Life** (EIUL) policy.

## BDs FORBID ADVISORS FROM SELLING EIUL POLICIES

Just like FIAs, many BDs forbid their securities licensed advisors from selling EIUL policies.

Why? I believe it's for the same reason they forbid advisors from selling FIAs. BDs and advisors make most of their money when selling an EIUL policy in the year of sale. Advisors are paid a decent sized commission in year one and the BD makes a small override on the product sale in year one. In years two-ten, there are very small renewal commissions paid to the advisors and insignificantly small overrides paid to the BD.

With a VUL, the advisor and the BD make money every year through trail fees. Actually, the larger the account balance in the VUL, the more money the advisor and the BD make.

In other words, EIUL policies do not fit in with the business model of a BD who wants to make ever increasing trail fees on assets under management.

What BDs do not allow their advisors to sell EIULs?

-Mass Mutual

-Northwestern Mutual

-State Farm

-MetLife

-New York Life

There are many others I'm sure who don't let their advisors sell EIUL policies, but I chose to list the above because these BDs are ones from companies that also manufacture/sell their own life insurance products. The above list of companies all sell whole life insurance policies and many have VUL insurance policies. None of them sell or offer internally an EIUL policy.

Why is this important? Because it's a doubly profitable situation if a securities licensed advisor with one of the above companies also sells a product offered by the parent or subsidiary company.

Would Mass Mutual rather have an advisor sell a Mass Mutual whole life or VUL policy or would it be more profitable to have a Mass Mutual advisor sell a life product from another company? Of course, Mass Mutual would rather have one of their own advisors sell a product offered by Mass Mutual

Let me remind you of the quote from a Mass Mutual advisor when he was answering my question about whether he could sell FIAs or EIUL policies:

"Even our outside brokerage operation will **not allow us to sell any indexed products**. Hope this helps."

## LACK OF DISCLOSURE IS WORSE THAN NOT BEING ABLE TO SELL FIAs

If you are not sufficiently outraged at what you've read so far, I want to cover again an issue that I find to be even more outrageous.

Sometimes reasonable minds differ as to what are the best products/tools that should be used to help clients of various ages in different financial situations.

Is it plausible that a BD that has hundreds if not thousands of advisors giving financial planning/retirement planning advice could fully research the value of EIUL policies decide that they are "all" bad products and are not ones that should be introduced to clients? I suppose so, although, from a mathematical standpoint it would be nearly impossible to come to such a conclusion.

Be that as it may, assume that a BD research department came to this conclusion; and, because of it, the compliance department decided to come down with a rule stating that no advisor licensed with the BD can sell EIUL policies.

One question that comes to mind is: Would a "good advisor" still take the time to research EIUL policies to determine if they are a product with any redeeming value for clients? The answer is yes. Only "bad advisors" take the word of their BD when it comes to research on products that could potentially be good for clients.

The most important question that needs to be asked and answered is whether or not an advisor who is forbidden from selling EIULs should disclose to a client that such products exist and further disclose that the advisor can't sell such products to the client because of the rules set forth by the BD.

The answer to this question is quite simple. For ANY advisor touting himself/herself as a financial planner or retirement planner (this includes anyone who is a CFP®), the answer is YES!

How can a financial planner who sells himself/herself to clients as someone with unique skills not disclose to a client that he/she can't sell a life insurance product for cash accumulation with the following attributes:

-the cash value never goes backwards due to stock market losses

-the gains are locked in annually (up to a cap)

-a free long-term care rider

-it can be issued with an optional guaranteed income rider that can be activated when the client is in retirement

How could an advisor look himself/herself in the face knowing that these products are out there; and, just because they made the mistake of hanging their securities license with the wrong BD, they can't sell such products or even discuss them with clients?

You want to know how most advisors look themselves in the face in spite of what you've read?

It's really simple—a high percentage of securities licensed advisors don't even know what an EIUL policy is, how it works, and that based on historical data, these policies would have significantly outperformed whole life, traditional universal life, and variable life insurance policies.

If you think I'm kidding, I'm not. If I had a dollar for every securities licensed advisor I've talked with over the last five years who told me they didn't know anything about EIUL policies, I'd be able to take several months off and vacation in the islands somewhere.

Why don't most securities licensed advisors know anything or very little about EIUL policies? You probably guessed it by now—the answer is because most look to their BD for education and product recommendations. If their BD forbids them from selling EIUL policies, they certainly are not receiving education about them.

I could respect to a point a securities-licensed advisor who discloses to a client up front that he/she can't talk about or sell EIUL policies and that the client might want to seek advice elsewhere before making a decision as to where to position money to grow wealth for retirement. I've never heard of an advisor making that disclosure; but if I did, I would not consider the advisor to be a "bad advisor."

## DISCLAIMER

I want to make it clear that neither this chapter nor this book opines on the stock or mutual fund picking ability of securities licensed advisors.

I am not qualified to review the seemingly endless amount of different money management platforms that securities licensed advisors use to help them decide where a client's money should be invested.

If you use a professional money manager or stock broker, it is possible that he/she is the best in the industry at picking for you stocks, mutual funds, and other types of investments.

## SUMMARY ON BAD IMOs AND BAD SECURITIES LICENSED ADVISORS

As I just stated, this book was not written to help you decide if your stock broker or financial planner is competent when it comes to picking stocks, mutual funds, etc.

This chapter is designed to point out the shortcomings of those advisors who are working with BDs that tie their hands and prevent certain securities-licensed advisors from providing the best advice to their clients. In other words, this chapter is designed to help you identify a "bad" securities licensed advisor who is incapable of giving complete advice on all the various options to help you grow your wealth in a protective and sometimes tax-favorable manner for retirement.

For review, the following are just some of the topics that some BDs forbid their advisors from discussing with and/or providing services to their client on:

1) <u>Life Settlements</u>—the sale of a life insurance policy of a client who is 65 or older. There are multiple reasons why various clients would want to sell their life insurance policy (can't afford it, need the cash to pay bills (including medical bills), want to profit from the sale and buy a better performing policy inside an irrevocable life insurance trust, etc.)

2) <u>Reverse Mortgages</u>—a special type of mortgage with no financial underwriting, no monthly payments, and no recourse outside of the value of the home. There are multiple reasons why a client 62 or older might want a RM (need cash to pay bills (including medical expenses) or to leverage the home in an effort to create more after-tax assets for the heirs in an estate plan).

3) <u>Fixed Indexed Annuities</u>—tax-deferred wealth-building tools that never have their values decline due to stock market losses, locks in gains every year, if any, can guarantee a return on an accumulation value of between 7-8% for 10-20 years (depending on the product) coupled with a guaranteed income for life that can never be outlived.

4) <u>Equity Indexed Universal Life Insurance</u>—a policy that has unique features such as the money never going backwards due to stock market losses, gains are locked in every year (up to a cap of 13-15%), a free long-term care rider, and even a guaranteed income rider for life that can be activated when in retirement.

Just ask yourself the question I've asked several times during this chapter: Would you rather take advice from an advisor who knew about, could discuss and help you buy, or use the above-listed products/concepts OR one who was forbidden by a BD from discussing and/or selling them?

Would you rather work with an advisor who, if he/she couldn't sell or deal with the above-listed products/concepts, discloses this fact to you up front so you could seek guidance elsewhere, OR would you rather deal with an advisor who withheld from you the fact the they were forbidden from discussing and/or selling them?

## WHAT IS A "BAD ADVISOR"?

A "bad advisor" is one who does not act in the best interest of his/her clients; and I would submit to you that, if you are dealing with an advisor who works with a BD that forbids them from selling or dealing with viable financial wealth-building, retirement, or estate-planning tools, you are working with a "bad advisor."

## QUESTIONS TO ASK YOUR SECURITIES LICENSED ADVISOR TO DETEMINE IF HE/SHE IS BAD

1) Are you a Registered Investment Advisor (RIA) and do you work under a Broker Dealer (BD)?

If the advisor answers yes to the first part of this question and no to the second, at least you know that advisor does not have his/her hands tied by the compliance department of a BD. That's no guarantee that the advisor will provide you the best advice, but it at least removes one of the obstacles.

2) Who is your BD (this will allow you to research if the BD uses an open or closed platform)?

3) Does your BD forbid you from selling and/or discussing anything (this is an open-ended question that will tell you a lot about the advisor depending on the answers)?

4) If the advisor doesn't answer the questions to your satisfaction, specifically ask the advisor about life settlements, reverse mortgages, FIAs, and EIULs.

If the answers to the above make it clear that the advisor has his/her hands tied by a BD, then you know it's not possible to receive unbiased advice from the advisor.

That means you may be counseled into products or investments that are not in your best interest and ones that will not accomplish your goals.

5) If your BD does not forbid you from giving advice on FIAs or EIUL policies, have you ever recommended one to a client?

Even if an advisor is not forbidden from dealing with FIAs or EIUL policies, it is important to you to know if the advisor has ever recommended one.

If you choose to work with an advisor notwithstanding the fact that he/she can't or won't give you the best unbiased advice possible, at least you have been forewarned and will have no one to blame if the outcome of the advice given does not match up with your goals.

# Chapter 5

## Financial Planners/CFPs®

I wanted to put in a brief chapter in this book on financial planners.

It seems to be a term that's thrown around by a lot of advisors who have no right in using the term.

This chapter will apply as well to Certified Financial Planners (CFPs®).

I took the following information directly from the Financial Planner Association's (FPA) website.

***What is Financial Planning?***

*"Financial planning is the long-term process of <u>wisely</u> managing your finances so you can achieve your goals and dreams, while at the same time negotiating the financial barriers that inevitably arise in every stage of life. Remember, financial planning is a process, not a product." (Emphasis added)*

I can't help but snicker a bit at the word "wisely" used in the FPAs definition of financial planning.

Additionally, did you notice the shot at insurance agents when in the definition the FPA stated that financial planning is a process, <u>not a product</u>?

There is a constant battle going on in the financial planning/insurance world between financial planners and insurance agents.

Financial planners have their securities license(s) (and typically an insurance license). Insurance agents "only" have their insurance license(s).

As you know from reading the chapter on Broker Dealers (BDs), only advisors licensed with the appropriate securities licenses can sell stocks, mutual funds, bonds, variable annuities, variable life insurance, etc.

Insurance-only licensed agents are limited to selling fixed products like Fixed Indexed Annuities (FIAs) and various fixed life insurance policies like Equity Indexed Universal Life (EIUL) insurance, disability insurance, long-term care insurance, etc.

For the most part, securities licensed advisors look down their nose at insurance-only advisors because they believe that only a financial planner with the right licenses can give "good" advice.

Insurance agents fight the stigma that they are product peddlers not problem solvers.

However, as you've read with clarity in this book, many times a securities licensed advisor gives more bad advice than an insurance-only licensed advisor could ever dream of giving.

As you will read in this chapter, just because someone is a financial planner or a Certified Financial Planner (CFP®), that is no guarantee that the advisor is able to give good advice or isn't what I call a "bad advisor."

The following is also from the FPA website discussing the process of how to help clients.

### ***Create a Sound Financial Plan***

*Step 1*

> *Establish Goals*

*Step 2*

> *Gather Data*

*Step 3*

> *Analyze & Evaluate Your Financial Status*

*Step 4*

> *Develop a Plan*

*Step 5*

> *Implement the Plan*

*Step 6*

> *Monitor the Plan & Make Necessary Adjustments*

It sounds great, doesn't it? Wouldn't you rather go to an advisor who has a structured and systematic way of working with clients in order to help them achieve their financial goals?

As you will read, having a systematic game plan for how to work with clients is totally irrelevant if the advisor you are dealing with has built-in biases that taints the advice given and simply doesn't know what he/she needs to know in order to give clients complete advice to help them grow and protect their wealth.

The following is also from the FPA website.

### *Why a CFP® Professional?*

*CFP® professionals are dedicated to using the <u>financial planning process</u> to serve the financial needs of individuals, families and businesses. Most CFP® professionals have earned a four-year college degree in a finance-related field, and have completed a course of study in financial planning approved by the CFP® Board. (Emphasis added)*

*To earn the prestigious CFP® certification and remain certified as a CFP® professional, individuals must meet four main requirements.*

*Certification Requirements:*

*Examination*

*CERTIFIED FINANCIAL PLANNER^TM Professionals must successfully complete CFP® Board's comprehensive certification examination, which tests an individual's knowledge on various key aspects of financial planning.*

*Experience*

*CERTIFIED FINANCIAL PLANNER^TM Professionals must acquire three years of financial planning-related experience before receiving the right to use the CFP® certification marks.*

*Ethics*

*CERTIFIED FINANCIAL PLANNER™ Professionals must voluntarily ascribe to CFP® Board's Code of Ethics and additional requirements as mandated. CFP® practitioners who violate the code can be disciplined, including permanent loss of the right to use the CFP® certification marks.*

*Education*

*CERTIFIED FINANCIAL PLANNER™ Professionals must complete 30 hours of continuing education every two years to stay current in financial planning knowledge, including ethics.*

*Compliance with these four areas informs you that an individual who holds the CFP® certification mark is well prepared and qualified to give sound, professional advice.*

Wow, the previous information sounds quite impressive doesn't it?

It almost makes me want to run out and find a CFP®.

You'll notice in the first sentence of this quote from the FPA site is the term <u>financial planning process</u>. It seems that the FPA really emphasizes the process as almost a failsafe way of helping advise clients appropriately when it comes to growing their wealth.

Don't get me wrong; I like processes. They help make sure advisors check the box to make sure items are discussed and evaluated so they are not missed and so an advisor is in the best possible position to give proper recommendations.

## WHAT'S WRONG WITH FINANCIAL PLANNERS OR CFPs®?

Let me get right to it since some of what I have to say is a bit redundant and is covered in other chapters.

### Built-in biases

It is clear that financial planners and CFPs® have built-in biases. Actually, all types of advisors have built-in biases. The key as a consumer is to understand them and to figure out how your advisor(s) deals with these biases to give you the best advice.

Financial planners have been taught that the best way to grow a client's wealth is through the "proper use of stocks, bonds, and mutual funds."

Some also use variable annuities.

Some also use variable life insurance.

Some also use real estate and several other types of investments.

However, these types of planners generally are NOT properly educated on the use of many fixed products such as Fixed Indexed Annuities (FIAs) and Equity Indexed Universal Life (EIUL) insurance. Without this education, it is impossible to give complete "financial planning" advice.

As you have read and will read more about, I believe that any advisor giving advice to clients on how to grow their wealth in a protective manner must know about FIAs and EIUL policies.

Why?

FIAs have the following qualities:

-Money never goes backwards due to stock mark losses.

-Gains are locked in every year and can never be lost.

-Some come with guaranteed returns of between 7%-8% on an accumulation value that rolls up between 10-20 years depending on the product.

-FIAs that come with guaranteed returns also couple those returns with a guaranteed income for life an annuity owner can never outlive.

EIUL policies have similar qualities:

-Money never goes backwards due to stock mark losses.

-Gains are locked in every year and can never be lost.

-Money grows tax-free (unlike an annuity that grows tax-deferred).

-Money can be removed tax-free to create a nice supplemental retirement income stream.

-One product even has a guaranteed income-for-life benefit.

-An EIUL policy is a self-completing, wealth-building tool. If you die before building wealth (unlike with a stock or mutual fund portfolio), a nice death benefit will be paid to your heirs that is equivalent to or greater than the wealth it would have taken you 10-20+ years to build.

It is my assertion that the vast majority of financial planners and CFPs® know very little, if anything, about FIAs and EIUL policies.

Why do I make such an assertion and how accurate is it?

I've been sending e-newsletters to over 150,000 securities licensed advisors for over six years (today my database is over 300,000). I've had many newsletters wherein I've stated without equivocation that I believe most financial planners and CFPs® violate their fiduciary duties to their clients because they don't know enough or anything about FIAs and EIUL policies.

When you send e-mails to such a large audience of advisors, many of whom believe they are the "best" planners in the industry, and tell them they are giving their clients terrible advice, it evokes a certain type of response.

What response? Many seem to have a need to tell me I'm wrong and try to do so in return e-mails or over a phone call. I have had several hundred phone calls with financial planners and CFPs® where I have had to defend my position that they do give "bad advice" if they don't know what they should about FIAs and EIUL policies.

## 33-PAGE WHITE PAPER

You know what one of my top downloads from advisors who receive my newsletter is? It's my 33-page white paper where I compare FIAs with guaranteed income riders to variable annuities with guaranteed income riders.

Why would the white paper be so popular?

It's simple. Most securities licensed advisors (financial planners and CFPs®) know very little if anything about FIAs. As you read in the BD chapter, many of them are forbidden from selling them or even discussing them.

They are downloading my white paper to learn more about FIAs (good for them), but many of them have told me they downloaded the white paper to go through my math so they could **prove me wrong**.

I don't blame them for wanting to prove me wrong. If everything I've ever been told is that FIAs are garbage that should not be sold (or can't be sold if you work with the wrong BD), I'd want to read a white paper that has math supporting the statement that FIAs with guaranteed income riders are better or much better than variable annuities with the same rider.

You know how many of the nearly 10,000 advisors who have downloaded that white paper have called me to tell me my math is wrong?

ZERO!

That should tell you a lot.

**WHAT ABOUT CASH VALUE LIFE INSURANCE?**

As you have and will read in this book, cash value life insurance can be one of the best ways to build wealth for retirement.

If properly designed, the "right" CVL insurance policy can grow more wealth for retirement than stocks, mutual funds, or bonds that are growing in a traditional brokerage account.

If properly designed, the "right" CVL insurance policy can grow more wealth for retirement than tax-deferred IRAs, 401(k)s, profit sharing plans, defined benefit plans, and even Roth IRAs or 401(k) plans.

This will sound counterintuitive to most, but the math is crystal clear. If you want to learn more about how to grow wealth properly using CVL insurance, you can go to www.badadvisors.com or you might want to pick up a copy of my book Retiring Without Risk (www.retiringwithoutrisk.com).

Are financial planners and CFPs® familiar with the concept of using CVL as a unique tax-favorable/wealth-building tool? Yes, almost all of them are.

However, you know what type of life insurance policy most financial planners and CFPs® recommend? Variable life insurance (VUL).

What's wrong with VUL policies? Nothing as long as you understand the pros and cons.

A VUL allows virtually unlimited growth in the policy. If the stock market returns 30%+, you can earn those returns in a VUL policy.

However, if the stock market crashes 59% like it did from the highs of 2007 to the lows of 2008, the cash in your policy goes down by the same amount (actually more due to the other costs).

A VUL, like stocks and mutual funds, is a risk/reward investment. There is nothing wrong with risky investments as long as you understand the risk and the alternatives available.

With an EIUL policy (which is a fixed policy that can be sold by life insurance advisors without a securities license), you can earn returns up to 15% annually with some policies (there is a cap) but money can NEVER go backwards due to stock market losses and the gains each year are locked in and can NEVER be lost due to stock market losses.

If financial planners and CFPs® decide that a CVL insurance policy is one of the tools that should be used to grow a client's wealth, do you think they should know something about EIUL policies?

I do and I consider financial planners and CFPs® that don't know a lot about EIUL "bad advisors."

As I state over and over in this book, it's not always about the advice an advisor can give, it's many times about how the limitations of the advice given are communicated to clients that makes a "bad advisor."

If a financial planner or CFP$^{®}$ disclosed to a potential client that he/she doesn't know anything about EIUL policies or FIAs and sets the expectation that the client will not receive advice about such products, then I would not consider the advisor a "bad advisor" (at least as it pertains to not giving advice about these products).

## REACHING YOUR FINANCIAL PLANNING GOALS

The term financial planning is pretty broad.

*"Financial planning is the long-term process of <u>wisely</u> managing your finances so you can <u>achieve your goals</u> and dreams, while at the same time negotiating the financial barriers that inevitably arise in every stage of life. Remember, financial planning is a process, not a product."*

I've never seen a definition that more fully describes "managing your finances so you can achieve your goals."

What are the goals of most people who seek advice from a financial planner?

It's different for different people.

It's different now than it was 10-20 years ago.

Even though this is a moving target, let me try to come up with a statement that will cover most people. How about the following: *Most clients want advice to grow their wealth in the **<u>least risky manner possible</u>** to reach their financial goals.*

What do you think? Is that reasonable? I want to reach my financial goals, and I don't want to take any more risk than is necessary to meet those goals.

For the sake of brevity and not to be too redundant, let me ask you one simple question:

If there were a product that could guarantee a return of 7%-8% on an accumulation value for 10-20 years that is coupled with a guaranteed income for life that could never be outlived, should a "financial planner" or certainly a CFP$^{®}$ know about these products?

Of course the answer is yes; but, again, many financial planners/ CFPs® know nothing about these products and many of them are forbidden by their broker dealers from selling them.

What's my point with this section? If you are looking to grow wealth in the "least risky manner possible to reach your financial planning goals," going to a "financial planner" or CFP® may not help you achieve your goals.

I could make the same analogy with growing wealth in a protective manner using equity indexed life insurance, but I think you get my point.

### TACTICAL MONEY MANAGEMENT (TMM)

Have ever heard the term TMM?

If you have money invested in the market (stocks, bonds, mutual funds, etc.) and you are getting advice from a "good" financial planner, you should be familiar with TMM.

Unfortunately, the vast majority of readers who have a "financial planner" will be unfamiliar with TMM. If you are one of them, you most certainly are dealing with a "bad advisor."

<u>What is TMM</u>? I found a really nice explanation of it on the internet.

Tactical Money Management Investing is an active and daily management style. One of the benefits is that it is daily in nature. In other words a tactical money manager will move between cash, assets classes, styles, segments or markets on a daily basis. The idea is that you want to take advantage of strengths in certain sectors while avoiding weaknesses in others. The approach will sometimes be "all in" or sometimes "all out" of the market and it is based on the analytical research and forecasts of the model. It is a **very effective way of managing risk**.

TMM is all about managing risk not reaching for returns with too much risk.

Let me ask you this: Which one of the following is the best investment?

-Investment 1 with a net return of 9%
-Investment 2 with a net return of 9%
-Investment 3 with a net return of 9%

They all had the same return, so how do you choose?

What if the following were the drawdown risk the investor would have to take on to achieve the net 9% rate of return?

-Investment 1 risks -4%
-Investment 2 risks -10%
-Investment 3 risks -20%

Now, which one would you prefer? Investment 1 with a 9% rate of return that only risks -4% of the investor's money?

Drawdown risk.: It is my belief that EVERY investor should be familiar with what I call drawdown risk (maximum loss from peak (high point of your investment during a given time frame) to valley (lower point of your investment during a given time frame)) when comparing investments. Why? Because most advisors pitching investments don't understand or talk about drawdown risk.

Did you know that the maximum **drawdown risk** of the S&P 500 going back to 2007 is **over 50%**?

Did you know that the maximum **drawdown risk** of an asset-allocated portfolio (also known as a "balanced" portfolio) going back to 2007 is **over 35%**?

If you had money invested with a CFP® the chances are nearly 100% that you had money in a stock index or an asset-allocated portfolio. If that was the case, then the -50% and -35% returns should look familiar.

Good TMM mitigates investment risk.

Because TMM seeks to avoid risk first, good TMM will significantly lessen your drawdown risk.

I found a Registered Investment Advisory (RIA) firm that specializes in finding top quality TMM strategies. The following are the numbers from the <u>top three conservative TMMs</u> going back to 2007 (numbers are year ending 2014)

<u>Maximum drawdown risk</u>: -7.82

-7.82% vs. -50% for the S&P and -35% for asset allocation.

I certainly like the much much lower drawdown risk of good TMM strategies better than indexing or asset allocation.

The question is do you have to sacrifice rate of return when using TMM?

It will depend on the managers of course, but the top three "conservative risk" managers of the RIA I recommend generated a **+9.19% "net" rate of return** going back to 2007.

How did the S&P do going back to 2007? **+7.27%**

How did an asset-allocated strategy do? **+5.5%**

What should the average investor like better? TMM with lower risk and better returns (keep in mind that past performance is no guarantee of future performance) or higher risk and lower returns?

The answer is obvious and if it is, why wouldn't a CFP® be offering several TMM strategies to clients? The simple and sad answer is most just don't know anything about TMM, and those that do don't know the ones I am citing in this book.

The end result is that clients of CFPs® and financial planners in general are taking far too much risk when trying to reach their investment goals.

Because readers who just read the previous few paragraphs should be outraged and upset at their current financial planners, I figured I'd add a little gas to the fire and give you the "moderate risk" managers for the top three TMM strategies at the RIA I recommend.

<u>Maximum drawdown risk</u>: **-18.88**

Average "net" rate of return going back to 2007: **+15.29%**

You'll notice that the "moderate risk" TMM strategies still have far less drawdown risk than the S&P or the typical asset-allocated portfolio, but have a much higher rate of return.

Again, I'll ask the simple questions, what do you like better? Lower risk and higher returns or higher risk and lower returns?

Not to be too redundant, but most CFPs® and most general financial planners do NOT use TMM to help their clients mitigate risk.

Finally, I wanted to explain why I took numbers going back to 2007. That's was when the last market crash happened. Every mutual fund and stock index looks great in an up market. From 2009-2014 the market has had a big upswing so nearly every investment did well.

It's not when the market is doing well that matters nearly as much as when it crashes. When it crashes, every investor will wish they had some or a significant amount of money in TMMs.

## BROAD OR NARROW KNOWLEDGE

When people work with a financial planner or especially a CFP®, many think that they are working with someone who has unique knowledge that will help the advisor provide the "best" advice possible.

It is true that CFPs® go through a lot of training to become CFPs®. Much of it is good training, and I commend them for that.

But the perception that a CFP® is some all-knowing advisor is a misnomer.

CFPs® are not taught the most important concept that all advisors who give advice about money should know. What's that? Asset protection.

The best financial plan in the world can be rendered meaningless unless it incorporates asset protection.

Because I have an entire chapter on the broad knowledge a "good advisor" should have in order to provide a comprehensive plan to help a client grow and protect their wealth, I will not go into it any further in this chapter.

## SUMMARY ON FINANCIAL PLANNERS/CFP®

There is nothing wrong per se with working with a financial planner or a CFP®. While you probably can't tell from this chapter, I like the fact that CFPs® go through additional training to try to better themselves and provide better advice.

However, the fact that someone is a "financial planner" or CFP® doesn't necessarily mean they are "good advisors" or, what's worse, it doesn't mean they are not "bad advisors."

As stated, many financial planners/CFPs® have a built-in bias against some of the most protective and useful wealth-building tools available.

This bias is very difficult for them to overcome (I know because I've been butting heads with them for years when discussing the value of FIAs and EIUL policies).

Each advisor you work with needs to be examined individually on their own merit. Just because advisors tout themselves as a financial planner or a CFP®, doesn't mean they are going to give you advice that will accomplish your financial/retirement planning goals.

## QUESTIONS TO ASK FINANCIAL PLANNERS OR CFPs® TO DETERMINE IF THEY ARE "BAD ADVISORS"

These are the same questions that I suggested you ask advisors in the chapter of this book where I discussed broker dealers (BD) and securities licensed advisors.

1) Are you a Registered Investment Advisor (RIA) and do you work under a BD?

If the advisor answers yes to the first part of this question and no to the second, at least you know that advisor does not have his/her hands tied by the compliance department of a BD. That's no guarantee that the advisor will provide you the "best" advice, but it at least removes one of the obstacles.

2) Who is your BD (this will allow you to research if the BD uses an open or closed platform)?

3) Does your BD forbid you from selling and/or discussing anything (this is an open-ended question that will tell you a lot about the advisor depending on the answer)?

4) If the advisor doesn't answer the questions to your satisfaction, specifically ask the advisor about life settlements, reverse mortgages, FIAs, and EIUL policies.

If the answers to the above make it clear that the advisor has his/her hands tied by a BD, then you know it's not possible to receive unbiased advice from the advisor.

That means you may be counseled into products or investments that are not in your best interest and ones that will not accomplish your goals.

5) If your BD does not forbid you from giving advice on FIAs or EIUL policies, have you ever recommended one to a client?

Even if an advisor is not forbidden from dealing with FIAs or EIUL policies, it is important for you to know if the advisor has ever recommended one.

6) Do you have access to TMM strategies?

7) If yes, what is the maximum drawdown risk of the TMM strategies you have access to going back to 2007?

8) If yes to 6), what is the average rate of return of the TMM strategies you have access to going back to 2007?

9) If yes to 6), what is the average percentage of assets you typically recommend be invested in TMM strategies?

If you are dealing with a financial planner who isn't very familiar with TMM strategies, has access to high quality TMM strategies, and actually recommends that his/her clients have a significant amount of money in these strategies, you certainly know you are working with a "bad advisor."

Finally, if you choose to work with an advisor who would clearly be labeled a "bad advisor" after ready this chapter, at least you have been forewarned and will have no one to blame if the outcome of the advice given does not match up with your investment/retirement goals.

# **Chapter 6**

## **Fee-Only Advisors**

This will be a short and simple chapter (although one that should offend you as much as any of the chapters in this book).

### **WHAT IS A FEE-ONLY ADVISOR?**

I went to the World Wide Web to find a handful of different explanations from the fee-only advisors themselves.

Quote #1

*"Fee-only advisors do <u>not</u> work for commission but rather earn a percentage of assets under management. This assures that your personal interests are served and that your advisor is not potentially swayed by any personal or corporate conflicts of interest."*

Quote #2

*"A fee-only financial advisor is one who is compensated <u>solely</u> by the client with neither the advisor nor any related party receiving compensation that is contingent on the purchase or sale of a financial product. Fee-only advisors may not receive commissions, rebates, awards, finder's fees, bonuses or other forms of compensation from others as a result of a client's implementation of the advisor's planning recommendations."*

Quote #3 (This is my favorite explanation I found on the Web).

*"What is Fee-Only Financial Planning?*

*Depending on the service you select, the fee is based on hourly fees, flat fees for financial plans, or asset management fees. There are **no** hidden fees or expenses, **nor** do we receive fees from third parties for the services recommended on behalf of our clients.*

*Your account will be customized using index funds, Exchange Traded Funds (ETFs), and "no load" or "load waived" mutual funds which put more of your investment dollars to work.*

### Why is Choosing a Fee-Only Advisor Important?

*Fee-only advice results in **objective advice** that meets your specific needs. Because we receive **no commissions of any kind**, or referral fees from accountants, attorneys, insurance professionals, or anyone else, we have no incentive to recommend a product or service unless it is in your best interest.*

### Other Forms of Compensation for Other Advisors

### What is a Commission-Based Advisor?

*A commission-based advisor receives commissions from financial companies for selling investments, insurance, and other financial products to their clients. The client may not see the commission, which can be paid in several ways, such as "loads," "12(b)1 fees," or sales incentives, but it is paid.*

### What is a Fee-Based Advisor?

*Fee-based advisors receive **both** commissions from product sales **and fees** from clients."*

Why do I like Quote #3 as my favorite? Because it's one that has the best marketing pizzazz. Why do I find that interesting? Because my assessment of fee-only advisors is that the concept that they give clients the best advice because they are fee-only is an oxymoron (a figure of speech that combines normally-contradictory terms).

Why do I use the term oxymoron? As I'll explain in this chapter, I think it's nearly impossible for a fee-only advisor to give the best unbiased advice to clients.

### FEE-ONLY IS GREAT MARKETING

When you read that fee-only advisors do not take commissions and because of this are in a position to always make recommendations that are in the client's best interest, it really makes sense, doesn't it?

As I stated in the chapter on "bad BDs and securities licensed advisors," many securities licensed advisors make the majority of their money from commissions (commissions that come from selling stocks and mutual funds).

The higher the turnover in a stock/mutual fund portfolio, the more money an advisor can make.

Additionally, advisors who make their money from selling products, many times will sell "loaded" products—ones that pay front-end and/or back-end commissions.

Therefore, it seems logical that, if consumers work with fee-only advisors, the advisors surely will be able to give less-biased advice, right? The advisor is on the same team as the client because the fee-only advisor makes money from an asset-based fee. The more the assets grow, the larger the annual fee the fee-only advisor makes.

This is great marketing in my opinion. I'm sure that most people reading this chapter have bought into it already and are wondering how I'm going to attack this platform and illustrate what makes a "bad" fee-only advisor.

## WHAT ABOUT FEE-BASED ADVISORS?

Let me talk briefly about fee-based advisors vs. fee-only advisors.

As stated earlier in Quote #3 that I pulled off the internet, a "fee-based" advisor can charge fees for advice given and earn money from commissions. If you've bought into the fee-only model as the only one that aligns an advisor's interest with that of his/her clients, then you probably think that a fee-based advisor must give tainted advice because they can earn commissions.

Actually, fee-based advisors are my favorite kind of advisors. If you want advice on securities products (stocks, mutual funds, variable annuities, etc.), fee-based advisors at least have the opportunity to give clients the "best" advice (I'll explain shortly).

## NO-LOAD LIFE INSURANCE AND ANNUITY PRODUCTS

What is a no-load life insurance or annuity product? It's one that doesn't pay a commission.

In theory, you'd think a product that doesn't have a commission must be better than those without, right? If an insurance company doesn't have to pay an agent to sell it, then the product must be priced better (term life insurance should be less expensive, cash value life insurance should have more cash, and annuities should have more cash and no or lower surrender charges).

There are a lot of things in life that sound good in theory but fail in the real world.

Over time, insurance companies have tried to roll out no-load or low-load insurance and annuity products.

Most of them were taken off the market. Why? They must have been better products, right?

No. Most of them were inferior products compared to the ones that paid commissions. How can that be?

Insurance companies put money into research and development of products they know will sell. As you'll find out, fee-only advisors know very little about most insurance products and, therefore, don't recommend or sell many of them.

If few advisors are selling no-load products, how long do you think an insurance company will keep them on the market? Right. Not very long.

You don't have to necessarily agree with what I'm saying, but what I'm saying is the truth.

Most of the good insurance and annuity products (except potentially some variable annuities) are commission-based products because there is a huge national sales force of licensed insurance advisors to sell them.

**WHAT MAKES A "BAD" FEE-ONLY ADVISOR?**

Let me just get right to the heart of the issue by asking you a few simple questions.

Do fee-only planners have a built-in bias against commission-based products?

Absolutely.

If fee-only advisors can't and won't offer commission-based products, what do you think the odds are of fee-only advisors knowing if any of the commission-based products are any good?

Nearly Zero!

How do I know? Because I've talked to dozens of fee-only advisors over the last several years who have proved their ignorance of commission-based products to me.

Why would I be talking with a fee-only advisor? I have thousands of them who receive the educational e-newsletters I send through The Wealth Preservation Institute. Many of them don't like the fact that I'm a strong advocate of insurance products such as Fixed Indexed Annuities (FIAs) and Equity Indexed Universal Life (EIUL) insurance.

I receive many negative e-mails and calls from fee-only advisors who tell me I'm doing the industry a disservice by touting the virtues of commission-based products.

It's like they are trying to convert me to the cult of fee-only planning.

However, unlike fee-only advisors, my ethical duty is to provide the best advice to my clients and counsel others to do the same no matter what products or concepts are on the table. If I think a commission-based product is the best, I'll recommend it. If I think a no-load product is the best, I'll recommend it.

Fee-only advisors have basically sworn an oath that is contradictory. Their oath is always to do the best for their client by NOT taking commissions. The problem with that as I've stated is that many of the best products in the market are commission-based products.

## EXAMPLE PHONE CALL TO EXPLAIN THE PROBLEMS WITH FEE-ONLY ADVISORS

Let me give you an example of the typical phone call I have from a fee-only advisor.

Advisor: Roccy, I read your newsletter the other day where you were bashing securities licensed advisors because you don't think they are doing right by their clients for various reasons.

Roccy: Hi, thanks for the call. Yes, I've done a number of articles indicating why many securities licensed advisors are giving bad advice to their clients.

Advisor: I wanted to call and tell you that I agree with much of what you say but that I also disagree with your insistence that many clients should build wealth with FIAs or cash value life insurance.

Roccy: Really? Why is that?

Advisor: As I'm sure you are aware, the products you talk favorably about in your newsletters are commission-based products.

Roccy: Yes, that's right.

Advisor: Well, as a fee-only advisor, my duty is to my client and to make sure my advice is not tainted by commissions. I am not allowed to sell commission-based products.

Roccy: You don't say.

Advisor: Yes. In fact, I've read your newsletters for several years now, and I usually think they are on point, creative, and very helpful when it comes to several topics. But you seem to have lost your way when it comes to recommending commission-based products.

Roccy: Really. Would you like me to comment on your position?

Advisor: Yes, I'm curious as to why you keep recommending commission-based products.

Roccy: Let me start by confirming that you do not sell products that pay commissions.

Advisor: Yes, that's correct.

Roccy: Would you say you know very much about the commission-based products that are out there?

Advisor: What do you mean?

Roccy: I wonder if you spend X amount of time each week researching commission-based products to make sure they are no good or not better than what you would otherwise offer them.

Advisor: Uh, no, I don't spend time researching commission-based products.

Roccy: Do you know what an FIA is?

Advisor: Sort of. It's some kind of an annuity, right?

Roccy: Yes, it's an annuity that never goes backwards, locks in gains every year, and can be purchased with a rider that guarantees a return of 6%-7% (on an accumulation value) coupled with a guaranteed income for life that a client can never outlive.

Advisor: Oh.

Roccy: Would you agree with me that a financial planner or Registered Investment Advisor (RIA) should know about any/all products that guarantee a return coupled with a lifetime income? Especially if the advisor is giving retirement planning advice.

Advisor: Yes (very hesitant usually because the advisor knows I'm now going somewhere specific with this discussion).

Roccy: I want to make sure I understand something. You tout yourself as an advisor who always puts the client's interest first because you do not make commissions; but you don't even know what an FIA is and certainly don't know anything about powerful FIAs that can guarantee a return of 7%-8% on an accumulation value that will be used to guarantee insureds an income for life they can't outlive.

Advisor: I suppose that's true.

Roccy: And will you admit that the reason you don't know anything about FIAs is because of your bias against insurance products that have commissions?

Advisor: Well, I'm not sure I'd put it that way. We just believe that clients, if they need to use annuity products, should use no-load products (ones without commissions).

Roccy: I get that. Do you know any no-load annuities that will guarantee a rate of return coupled with guaranteed income for life a client can't outlive?

Advisor: No.

Roccy: Let me ask you this. What kind of investments do you recommend for clients who are 65 or older who are scared of losing money in the stock market and who want to make sure they have a guaranteed income that will never run out before they die?

Advisor: Well, I would typically recommend no-load mutual funds and maybe bonds or whatever else made sense for the client.

Roccy: You mean you are going to recommend a "proper mix of stocks, mutual funds, bonds, etc.?"

Advisor: Yes, but ones with no commissions.

Roccy: Right, I get that; however, there is no guarantee with the investments you recommend to clients, and your projected returns are simply a guess as to what you think the investments will do over time. If those projections don't come true, your clients will run out of money in retirement.

Advisor: Well, we have investment models we use to mitigate that risk.

Roccy: Really? Most elderly clients are not interested in mitigating risk if there are options to eliminate it.

Roccy: Let me ask you about the advice you give to your clients who are under the age of 55.

Advisor: Ok.

Roccy: What do you think about using cash value life insurance as an asset class and as a tax-favorable/wealth-building tool for retirement?

Advisor: Life insurance as a wealth-building tool? No. I don't recommend using life insurance as a wealth-building tool.

Roccy: Why (of course, I already know the answer before he answers it because I've heard it from dozens of other fee-only advisors)?

Advisor: Why? Because life insurance is a terrible place to build wealth. There are good-sized commissions that are paid in most products, and then there are the insurance expenses that are a drag on cash growing in the policy.

Roccy: How familiar are you with Equity Indexed Universal Life (EIUL) insurance?

Advisor: I've never heard of it.

Roccy: What are you familiar with?

Advisor: Whole life, variable life, and universal life.

Roccy: Then is it fair to say that you've not run numbers to determine if EIUL policies will work as a tax-favorable and protective wealth-building tool?

Advisor: Yes.

Roccy: Will you agree with me that a properly structured policy allows cash to grow tax-free and come out tax-free?

Advisor: Yes.

Roccy: What if I told you that various EIUL policies over the last twenty years have averaged anywhere from 7.2% in excess of 9% (depending on the policy used)?

Advisor: Really?

Roccy: Would you become more interested in EIUL policies if you knew the money in the policy could never go backwards due to stock market losses?

Advisor: Yes.

Roccy: Would you become more interested if you knew the gains in the policy were locked in at the end of every year and could never be lost due to stock market losses?

Advisor: Yes.

Roccy: Would you become more interested to learn that from 1998-2008 the stock market averaged a negative 1.45% and that many of the EIUL policies in the market returned close to 6%?

Advisor: Yes.

Roccy: If you want to learn more about EIUL policies and why they can be a terrific protective tax-favorable/wealth-building tool, you should pick up a copy of my book, Retiring Without Risk. In my book, I explain how EIUL policies can work out as better or much better wealth-building tools than stocks, mutual funds, and bonds and even tax-deferred 401(k) plans. Also, in the book, I cover FIAs and FIAs with guaranteed income riders. I highly recommend you pick up a copy of the book.

Advisor: I might do that.

Roccy: Right, but just for the record, even if you determined that an EIUL policy or an FIA were the "best" option for a client, you couldn't sell one to a client because you are a fee-only advisor.

Advisor: No. I could counsel the client to buy one; but I just couldn't make any money from the sale because I can't make money from commission products.

Roccy: Right. And there's the rub. You actually have a disincentive to learn about commission-based products because you can't make money selling them. Besides your built-in and inaccurate bias against all commission-based products, you actually have a conflict of interest when taking a stance that you won't make money from commissions.

The conflict being that, if you were to recommend the best product or wealth-building tool for a client that happened to be a commission-based product (which will never happen because you don't know anything about commission-based products), you wouldn't make any money. Do you see the conflict?

Advisor: No.

Roccy: No? You don't see a conflict when providing the best advice puts you in a position to make no money? There is no conflict between what's best for you and what's best for your clients?

Advisor: I see your point, but I always recommend the best investments for my clients. As a fee-only advisor, I am the only type of advisor who can give unbiased advice because I don't make money on the sale of products.

Roccy: Our conversation has already proved the point that you are not capable of providing your clients the best advice because you have a built-in bias against commission-based products. Not only do you have a built-in bias, but you have an admitted ignorance of many of the best commission-based products.

Advisor: I don't agree with that.

Roccy: I'd expect no other stance from you.

I appreciate the call today. I'll chalk it up to yet another bang-my-head-against-the-wall call with a fee-only advisor who is under the false impression that commission-based products are bad or evil and who is not willing to take the time to research and understand commission-based products to make the decision if they really can be of value to clients.

Advisor: Good day.

Roccy: Good day.

## SUMMARY OF THE PREVIOUS PHONE CALL

First, let me state the previous phone call is one I have several times a year. Fee-only advisors are very consistent in their point of view and how they conduct their business.

What can be learned from the previous call?

1) That fee-only advisors know very little about most commission-based products (because they can't sell them and make money from them, there is no incentive to spend time learning them).

2) That fee-only advisors have an admitted built-in bias against commission-based products.

3) That most fee-only advisors know nothing or very little about FIAs and EIUL policies (mathematically two of the best wealth-building/retirement-planning tools available).

4) That fee-only advisors have the ability to recommend commission-based products but can't sell them themselves.

5) That fee-only advisors cannot possibly provide the best unbiased advice to their clients. In fact, it's just the opposite for many clients because of their built-in biases and limitations.

## ONE MORE EXAMPLE OF THE PROBLEMS WITH FEE-ONLY ADVISORS

Let's assume that a fee-only advisor has a client who is 60-years old and has $500,000 of the money in his IRA. The client is scared of the stock market and has as his number one goal to never run out of money in retirement.

If the client used one that rolled up a **guaranteed return at 8%** for ten years and then turned on his **guaranteed income for life**, the account value for income purposes at age 70 would be **$1,187,409** and the guaranteed income for life payment (which is not an annuitized payment) would be **$71,245** (this product also had a 10% up-front bonus that helped drive up the values).

Of course, the fee-only advisor can't find any way to guarantee such income from a "properly balanced mix of stocks, mutual funds, and bonds" without using an FIA.

The question is: Is the fee-only advisor really going to recommend that this client use an FIA to grow wealth and guarantee an income for life?

The real-world answer is NO WAY.

Why? Call me a cynic; but, if the advisor recommends an FIA to this client, he will be losing $5,000 a year on average as a fee that he charges on the assets he currently has under management.

Let's expand the example. Assume the fee-only advisor has 20 clients over the age of 60 who have the same fears and goals. Assume the total wealth of these clients is $10,000,000 that could arguably be repositioned into FIAs.

Assume the fee-only advisor charges a 1% fee annually to manage the money for these 20 clients. That means the advisor makes $100,000 in fees on these clients.

Is it reasonable to think that a fee-only advisor who has seen the light when it comes to growing wealth in a protective and guaranteed manner with FIAs is going to counsel his clients to move their money to an FIA? To many the question is laughable. Again, there is no way a fee-only advisor is going to move money to an FIA that he/she doesn't make money on.

Is it possible a fee-only advisor could still charge a fee to manage the FIAs? It's possible, but what's the point? Once the money is growing at 7%-8% a year guaranteed on the accumulation value and since the client already knows from day one what the guaranteed income will be at any age, why would a client pay a fee to an advisor to give advice going forward on these products? They wouldn't.

**FEE-BASED PLANNERS**

Let me discuss a little more about fee-based planners (vs. fee-only planners).

Fee-based planners are ones who can make commissions on clients but who typically use no-load mutual funds and other low-load investments for clients when dealing with typical brokerage account money.

Why do I like fee-based planners?

Because they too are on the side of their clients when it comes to asset-based fees vs. commissions that are made when buying and selling stocks, mutual funds, and bonds.

However, if the fee-based advisor understands the value of cash value life insurance or fixed indexed annuities, he/she can recommend either product and make money from the advice given.

Fee-based planners have an incentive to learn about commission-based products so the best advice can truly be given to clients (unlike fee-only advisors who have no incentive to learn about commission-based products).

## SHOULD YOU NEVER USE A FEE-ONLY ADVISOR?

This is a great question. If it were me, the answer would be that I would never use a fee-only advisor. Is it because I think they are all dishonest or incapable of giving money-management advice?

No. It's because the vast majority of them know nothing or very little about commission-based products; and even if they did know something about them, there is a disincentive to recommend them to clients.

Because of my research on FIAs and EIULs, I know mathematically that for many clients they can be two of the best tools to grow wealth in a protected manner.

It would be very difficult to think that an advisor who knows nothing about these products and, in fact, has taken an oath not to make money from these products (which is equivalent to taking an oath not to recommend these products) can give the "best" advice to me or to anyone else.

## QUESTIONS TO ASK A FEE-ONLY ADVISOR TO DETERMINE IF HE/SHE IS A "BAD ADVISOR"

These are questions that you'll already know the answer to before asking them.

1) Are you a fee-only or fee-based advisor?

If the answer is fee-only, then you know he/she has the issues discussed in this chapter.

2) Do you know what an FIA is?

3) Do you know what an EIUL policy is?

4) Do you regularly research FIAs and EIUL policies to make sure you are up to date on the best ones in the market at any given time?

4) Have you ever recommended either to your clients?

5) Would you recommend an FIA or EIUL policy to me if you thought it was the best way for me to grow wealth in a protective manner?

Again, you should already know the answers to the previous questions before you ask them; and, if that is the case, you may choose to simply make sure that the advisors you work with are NOT fee-only advisors.

# Chapter 7
## Sales Systems

What comes to mind when you think of the term "sales system?"

You might think about Amway or Prepaid Legal. Both are successful, multi-level marketing systems that also carry with them a negative stigma.

I'm sure that most readers of this book have been pitched some kind of sales system during their lifetime.

### WHAT IS A SALES SYSTEM?

Before I give you my definition, let's look at some of the definitions that relate to professional selling from Wikipedia:

*Marketing is defined as an ongoing process of planning and executing the marketing mix (Product, Price, Place, Promotion) for products, services or ideas to create exchange between individuals and organizations.*

*Advertising is defined as a form of communication that typically attempts to persuade potential customers to purchase or to consume more of a particular brand of product or service.*

*Public relations is defined as the practice of managing the flow of information between an organization and its audiences.*

*Sales Promotions is defined as the pre-determined actions designed to increase consumer demand, stimulate market demand or improve product availability for a limited time (i.e., contests, point of purchase displays, rebates, free travel, and sales incentives).*

I found the following useful information on the internet that was posted by Dr. Brian Lambert. Some of the following will make logical sense, and some will make little sense. While it might not make a lot of sense to you, what you should take away from reading it is that the sales process can be a highly refined one by marketing entities using psychology to their advantage to make sales (sales many times at all costs (which many times is to the detriment of the client buying the services or product)).

*"The sales process refers to a systematic process of repetitive and measurable milestones, the definition of the sales "profession" doesn't exist (until now with this article).*

*The following three tenets are required for professional selling:*

*-The focus of the sales profession centers on the human agents involved in the exchange between buyer and seller.*

*-Effective selling requires a systems approach, at minimum involving roles that sell, enable selling, and develop sales capabilities.*

*-A specific set of sales skills and knowledge are required to facilitate the exchange of value between buyers and sellers.*

*Within these three tenets the following definition of professional selling is offered by the American Society of Training and Development (ASTD):*

### *Professional Selling is:*

*"The holistic business system required to effectively develop, manage, enable, and execute a mutually beneficial, interpersonal exchange of goods and/or services for equitable value."*

*Note: this definition was published by ASTD in 2009.*

*What does this definition accomplish?*

*First, it creates a definition of world class selling. An organization wishing to benchmark its selling effectiveness can leverage the above definition to clearly understand strengths and weaknesses. Without such a definition, most adjustments to the selling team are arbitrary and subjective. By understanding the system's view required for selling effectiveness, organizations can look at individual sales team members as well as sales team processes and tools and how they align to the buyer.*

*Second, it allows for more consistent results in performance through the clear establishment of roles regarding who is "in" and who is "out" of professional selling. For example, if it doesn't involve a human agent, it is not within the sales profession -- it's a marketing function with a transaction (i.e., a "sale"). For this definition, sales operations, sales recruiters, and sales trainers are "in" the profession because they possess unique skills outside of their regular job titles. They possess knowledge and skill that is unique to enabling the definition.*

*Third, the definition lays the foundation for sales talent management/people strategies. With such a definition, sales development employees can create learning solutions that fit the unique aspects of a sales culture. At the same time, front-end recruitment strategies more clearly tie to retention strategies.*

*Fourth, it helps organizations on exemplary performance. By setting a bar with such a definition, organizations don't have to settle for mediocre sales effectiveness. They can use the definition to help bridge the gap between sales capacity and sales team competency."*

Again, the point of putting the previous information in this book is to make sure you understand that many of the advisors trying to sell you their services or products are using a "selling system."

The system may have costs tens of thousands if not hundreds of thousands or even millions of dollars to refine. However, once a sales process has been refined, it is used in a repetitive manner to make sales because it's been proven to work.

## WHAT'S MY LAYPERSON'S DEFINITION OF SALES SYSTEMS?

A sales system is a tested and repeatable process that is used to allow a salesperson the best opportunity to make maximum sales. The goal of a sales system is NOT to provide the best advice to clients. Instead, a sales system is one that is seller-centered, not client-centered. Sales systems are about making sales, not providing the consumer what they need.

Sales systems use any means necessary to make the sale. That means using tested psychological ploys to motivate an unwilling buyer to buy.

The tools used in a sales system will vary and can be very diverse. A sales system could be based off of a bestselling book (one written for the sole purpose of being part of a sales system and creating a sales force).

A sales system in the life insurance and annuity market many times will involve illustration software, charts, graphs, etc., to help the salesperson close the deal.

Essentially, sales systems are prevalent in all industries for one simple reason. They work.

### ARE ALL SALES SYSTEMS BAD?

No. Just because someone is using a sales system to educate and motivate clients doesn't mean the system or the advice or product sold, is bad (although it increases the likelihood that the advice is bad).

Whether a sales system is bad will be determined by the product sold and the manner in which an advisor can deviate from the system to provide unique/custom advice to clients.

If the products sold through a sales system are bad, then there is no remedy to fix the system; and I would consider the system a bad system (not because someone can't make sales, but because the end consumer is being sold an inferior or even defective product that they shouldn't be purchasing).

If the products being sold through a sales system are good or if the advisor using the system has the ability to choose the best products for each individual client that best fits their need, then the system wouldn't inherently be bad.

However, even if the advisor using the system has the ability to pick the very best products for each individual client, if buying even a good product is still NOT in the client's best interest, the system is still a bad system. Why? Because it works too well and helps create sales of products to clients who should not be buying them (even if the products themselves are good products).

## SALES SYSTEMS IN THE FINANCIAL SERVICES/INSURANCE INDUSTRY

As I've stated a few times in this book, the main focus of this book is to identify "bad advisors" in the life insurance and annuity field as well as financial planners who manage money or sell stocks, mutual funds, and bonds.

Wouldn't you know it, most of the sales systems out there, and the ones I'll talk about in this book, were created to sell life insurance and/or annuities.

What systems will I be covering?

-Missed Fortune 101® and Stop Sitting on Your Assets®
-UFirst®
-LEAP®
-College planning
-Infinite Banking System® (also known as Bank On Yourself (BOY) or Become Your Own Banker (BYOB))

My goal is not to make you an expert and dissect each one of these sales systems. I will tell you a little about each system, what I think it's trying to accomplish, and what I think is wrong with each.

Hopefully, with the information you'll read, you'll be armed to ask good questions of anyone who uses these or other sales systems so you can determine if you are dealing with a "bad advisor" who is more interested in selling than what's in your best interest.

## MISSED FORTUNE 101® AND STOP SITTING ON YOUR ASSETS®

These two systems are oldies but not goodies in my opinion.

Missed Fortune 101® (MF101) and Stop Sitting on Your Assets® (SSOYA) are both books.

What kind of books? It depends on whom you ask. You can find them on Amazon and buy them yourself. So some think they are simply educational books the general public can use to learn how to grow wealth in a secure and tax-favorable manner.

If you ask someone in the life insurance industry, they will most likely tell you that they are sales books to help insurance agents sell life insurance (which has turned out to be true).

What is the concept behind both books?

It's a timeless concept revolving around using other people's money to grow wealth.

Specifically, both books tell readers why it's a good idea to maximize the debt on a personal residence to grow your wealth.

The sales pitch goes something like this: If you could borrow money that cost you a net 4% and reposition that money into an asset where the money could grow at 7-8% tax-free, would you do it?

If you put pen to paper to figure out the math behind the above question, the answer would be an enthusiastic YES!

Both books, however, have several flaws when it comes to the math provided. Additionally, both books incorrectly deal with the tax code and the ability to deduct home equity debt.

I was so offended by the lack of accurate information in these sales books that I wrote my own book explaining the concept of borrowing money from your home to build wealth (The Home Equity Management Guidebook: How to Achieve Maximum Wealth with Maximum Protection).

I also created two websites where I break down sections of both books and tell readers what's wrong with them: www.www-missedfortune101.com; and www.www-stopsittingonyourassets.com

Because I literally have two full websites that discuss the problems with both books, I will not elaborate on the problems in this book.

National sales forces—both authors of these books have created national sales forces of licensed insurance agents to sell clients the concepts discussed in each book.

The author of <u>MF 101</u> had the gumption to charge agents $3,000-$5,000 to be trained in the concepts covered in his book. I thought this was novel considering the book teaches certain concepts in a manner that does not comply with the tax code or uses what I call "fuzzy math" to make the sale.

Has it worked? Have advisors been able to use these books to make life insurance sales? Unfortunately, the answer is yes. Hundreds of agents have been able to use these books as a sales platform to educate and motivate clients to borrow money from their houses to fund cash value life insurance.

What you might find interesting is that there have been a number of lawsuits filed against agents who have counseled clients to borrow money and reposition that money into cash value life insurance. Because of this, many insurance companies specifically forbid licensed insurance agents from selling life insurance to clients if the premium has been borrowed.

In any event, while the number of advisors using these books has dwindled over the years, the books and sales systems behind both have been a staple in the insurance industry for years; and now you have been forewarned that an advisor using either one of these books to motivate you to buy life insurance is what I would call a "bad advisor."

## UNITED FIRST FINANCIAL (U1st)

The story behind this sales platform is very interesting. I'll try to be brief.

I received a call from one of the two principals of U1st back in 2006. He wanted to introduce me to a wonderful "opportunity" to become a millionaire. I figured he was full of it, but that's a call I had to at least entertain.

He told me about this new program he and his partner had rolled out that would revolutionize the mortgage industry. It was a program that could help clients pay off their mortgage 5-10-15+ years early without changing their lifestyle.

It was not a bi-weekly program or anything else that had traditionally been used in the United States mortgage industry.

He said he was bringing over the principals of a company called Primerica to their business model of recruiting advisors to sell the program (to learn about Primerica, just Google Primerica and scam and you'll get pages of interesting reading).

This mortgage acceleration program worked through a unique one-of-a kind <u>software application,</u> and that is how U1st was going to make its money and help advisors like me make millions.

The retail price of the mortgage acceleration software was $3,500 (I'm not sure if they still charge this amount). The sales pitch to clients was that the software is what makes the program work (giving the allusion that the program won't work without it).

Let me just explain the sales tree, and I think you'll understand the system.

At the top of the pyramid is the main company U1st. The company has top level sales people (call them level one) who recruit other advisors (call them level two) to start selling this mortgage acceleration program.

When a level-two advisor sells a client the $3,500 mortgage acceleration program, he/she gets to keep, let's say, $650 from each of the first five sales, $1,200 from the next X amount of sales, and then up to $2,500 per sale after Y amount of sales have been made (these numbers are just for example purposes and may not be the exact numbers used by U1st).

The remainder of the money from the sale goes up the pyramid. The level-one recruiter makes X amount from every sale made by a level-two advisor and the remaining goes up the pyramid to the corporate owners.

These pyramids typically go about six to seven levels deep.

Because there is so much power in being able to sit down with clients to show them how to save tens of thousands if not hundreds of thousands of dollars by using this program, advisors pitching this program have had a significant amount of success.

## WHAT'S THE PROBLEM? WHAT'S WRONG WITH THIS SALES PLATFORM?

Let me tell you the rest of the story.

I was familiar with this mortgage acceleration program because I read a book explaining how it works about twelve months before I received the call from one of the owners of U1st.

I learned from a $25 book how the program worked and how simple it was to implement without software or third-party help. The program came out of Australia, made its way through Europe, and, finally, made its way to the U.S. back in about 2005.

The program NEVER had software until the two creative founders of U1st came out with their $3,500 software package and multi-level compensation program for agents who wanted to either sell the program or recruit people to sell it underneath them.

### MY OWN PROGRAM

I was so put off by my call with the co-founder of U1st that after the call I decided to create my own mortgage acceleration software and write my own book describing how the program works.

I created the software not to sell to the general public but instead so advisors could run the numbers and help their clients see the power of the program.

My program is called the Home Equity Acceleration Plan (H.E.A.P.™) (which is also the name of the title of my book that explains specifically how the program works). You can learn about H.E.A.P.™ at www.heaplan.com, and you can learn about the non-profit I have that goes along with the program at www.heaplan.org.

So far you might find the story about U1st and H.E.A.P.™ interesting, but why is it in this book? Yes, it's easy to say that someone selling a software package that is not needed for $3,500 to clients who have no idea that the software is not needed obviously qualifies someone as a "bad advisor."

However, this book is mainly about the financial services and insurance industry and identifying "bad advisors" which I will now elaborate on.

### U1st INSURANCE SALES

If you look, what you'll find is that it's a pretty small circle out there when it comes to creative life insurance and annuity sales techniques.

I alluded to Primerica earlier. Primerica is a company that helps advisors sell financial and insurance products. As I stated, the founders of U1st seemed to be building their business based on the Primerica model.

This seemed to be proven true when I was forwarded marketing material from a U1st agent who was using a U1st platform to sell life insurance and annuities.

Was that the original intent of the founders of U1st? To create an army of advisors to sell their $3,500 software packages and then turn them into a life insurance sales force? Who knows, but that's what seems to have happened.

What you might find interesting is that I've seen U1st agents pushing another concept you'll see in this chapter (The Infinite Banking System). This is amazing and a sad commentary on advisors who get sucked into using these systems to make a living.

### CONCLUSION ON U1st

The mortgage acceleration concept is a sound one. It's a great concept if you don't have to pay $3,500 for software you don't need.

The conclusion that is easy to draw from this book is that, if you are dealing with someone selling a $3,500 mortgage acceleration plan (whether they are trying to sell you the program itself or life insurance, annuities, or any other type of product), you are dealing with what I would call a "bad advisor."

## LEAP SYSTEMS®

What is LEAP?

The following is from the LEAP website:

*LEAP is an "Innovative Financial Simulator that allows professionals and their clients to understand financial issues and opportunities under a variety of economic conditions."*

*LEAP helps you "understand the cost of common financial strategies and how to recapture those cost to create greater wealth and benefits."*

*LEAP is a "simple, user-friendly interface which is highly visual and appeals to a variety of clients."*

*LEAP "uses financial modeling, calculators, graphs, and tables to create dynamic client presentations."*

What do I think LEAP is?

I view it as a program that is designed to help insurance agents communicate the value of cash value life insurance as a wealth-accumulation/retirement vehicle and manipulate the client through various software outputs to move forward with a purchase.

It's a sales system that is highly refined.

It's also quite complicated to use (or it was when I tried the software some years ago).

Actually, when I sat down to write this chapter, I couldn't come up with a good way of describing what LEAP really does.

Here is my attempt.

LEAP has many inputs an advisor can use to fill out a client's financial profile. It can be very specific and can accommodate inputs as insignificant as the deductible on your homeowners insurance.

Once a client's data has been entered into the LEAP system, you can have it create any one of dozens of different outputs that can be used to educate and motivate a client to purchase cash value life insurance as a wealth-building tool.

## WHAT'S WRONG WITH LEAP?

There is nothing wrong per se with the LEAP software. I personally don't like it because it's too hard to use, and I don't like sales presentations that average 10-15 outputs. Most clients won't understand half of them and, ultimately, will be buying something because they trust the agent vs. understanding the multiple outputs.

My biggest gripe with LEAP is the products that are typically recommended by LEAP licensed advisors. The person who started the LEAP system seems to be stuck in the 1980s when the program was created and product options were limited.

Virtually every LEAP licensed advisor I've ever talked with uses whole life insurance when selling a policy to a client using this system.

While I don't have time to cover it in this book in any detail, it is my opinion that whole life insurance is not the best policy to grow a tax-favorable nest egg for retirement. Whole life is the most expensive kind of life insurance a client can purchase, and the upside growth is significantly limited due to the policy design.

My preference would be to have LEAP licensed advisors recommend what I call Retirement Life™. It's a type of Equity Indexed Universal Life (EIUL) insurance policy. Mathematically and historically tested, EIUL policies have and should continue to significantly outperform whole life policies.

But, again, if you sat across the table from a LEAP licensed advisor, the chances are nearly 100% that the advisors when making his/her ultimate recommendation to you will recommend whole life.

## ARE LEAP LICENSED ADVISORS "BAD ADVISORS?"

Not by definition. Again, there is nothing per se wrong with the LEAP software. However, advisors who are brainwashed to sell one type of life insurance policy as a wealth-building tool and only one type of policy are what I consider "bad advisors."

Would I recommend you use a LEAP licensed advisor?

Not really. The ones I've talked with seem to be slaved to the software and whole life. Advisors who take as gospel the word/recommendation of a software program instead of independently being able to come up with their own recommendations are not the type of advisors I would recommend to a client.

Again, does that mean all LEAP advisors are "bad advisors?" No. I do know some who simply use the software as needed to run numbers to help the advisor come up with his/her own unique wealth-building plan for clients.

## COLLEGE-PLANNING SYSTEMS

For this section of the material, I'm not going to pick on any one particular sales system. I'm instead going to talk about two different sales tracks advisors take when dealing with helping clients with college planning.

Let me first answer the question: Why would a financial planner or insurance agent want to deal with "college planning?"

It's interesting, but there are several sales systems out there advisors can use to try to pick up new clients that focus on college planning.

The number one reason that an advisor will start marketing himself/herself as a college planner is to occupy space in a niche market in their local community on what I'll call a "motivational" subject matter—the key being a motivational subject matter.

If a financial planner comes to you and asks you if you would like to sit down to discuss your finances, what are you going to say? Probably that you are not interested.

Now assume you have a child who is age 5-17 and the advisor says to you, "I'd like to sit down with you and help you figure out the most economical way to send your child to college." This could be by helping the child receive financial aid, or it could be by using "special" wealth-building tools to save for college.

Now what would you say? The chances of you telling the advisor you'd be happy to meet with him/her should increase dramatically. This is why many advisors become "college planners."

## TWO COLLEGE PLANNING MARKETING PLATFORMS

When I researched what was going on in the college-planning space a few years ago, I came to the conclusion there were two types of marketing platforms.

Platform #1 is geared towards charging clients fees to help them find financial aid for students and to help them get accepted to the college of their choice.

Platform #2 is geared toward helping students financially qualify for aid by repositioning the assets of their parents and by helping them save money for college in what are called non-countable assets.

### Let me discuss Platform #1 first

Would you pay $1,000 to $5,000 if an advisor could help your son or daughter get into the school of his/her choice? Would it help if the advisor was also able to find significant financial aid to help pay for your child's education?

I can tell you the answer is yes, because I know there are many advisors who make a living charging clients a fee to help them with these issues.

What's wrong with Platform #1?

Nothing if the advisor you are working with is providing value for his/her services. However, what I can tell you is that certain clients, no matter what they do, will not be able to help their children receive financial aid.

Two kinds of financial aid: need-based and merit-based. "Rearranging" a family's financial situation has been used to sell products by uninformed and unscrupulous advisors trying to game the college planning system to help clients get need-based aid.

For example, the number one factor to determine if children are going to receive financial aid is the income of their parent(s). If that income is in excess of $90,000, the chances of a child receiving financial aid from a public institution are usually slim.

But the college planner told you that he/she had some magic process and way to help your child receive financial aid. Is that possible? I suppose. To me it's more like an urban legend. I've heard from an advisor who heard about an advisor who was able to find financial aid for a child whose parents made $150,000 a year. I've just never talked with someone for whom it actually worked.

For the most part, advisors who charge fees to help clients are banking on the hope factor. Advisors know that, if they float their services out to enough potential clients, X amount of them will purchase them at $1,500-$2,500+ for help to try to find aid for a student to go to college.

My warning when dealing with an advisor who is pitching fee-based services is simply "buyer beware." If you want to give it a shot, that's your prerogative; but if you make more than $75,000-$90,000 a year, you may be throwing good money away that could be used to help pay for your child's education.

**What kind of an advisor would be a "bad advisor" pitching Platform #1?**

One who oversells his/her ability to help (and they all say there is no guarantee so such a disclosure would not remove the tag of "bad advisor").

**Platform #2 is really the reason I started educating advisors on "proper" college planning.**

Platform #2 is one used by life insurance agents to sell life insurance to clients who hope that funding life insurance will either help qualify their child for aid or will work as a nice tax-favorable, college-savings tool.

Let me first address how to use cash value life insurance as a tool to help a student qualify for aid.

Assume you earn $95,000 a year. You have a child who is 16-years old and will be applying for college in the near future.

When the student fills out the Free Application for Federal Student Aid (FAFSA) form, the assets and income of the parents will be listed. (The FAFSA form is one your child would fill out and send in in hopes of receiving financial assistance when going to college).

When a client sits down with a "college planner," he/she will look at a family's assets and will tell clients who have too many assets that they need to be "repositioned" in order to have the child be in the best possible position to receive aid.

Therefore, if you have $100,000 in a brokerage account, that is considered a "countable" asset for aid calculation purposes.

You know what's not currently a countable asset? Cash value life insurance. That's right; you've probably already guessed what the college advisor is going to tell clients. He/she will tell this example client to cash in the brokerage account and fund a single premium life insurance contract before the student applies for aid.

This is called asset repositioning, and it can work if your child is applying to a public school (some private schools have caught onto the trick-and-treat cash value life insurance as a countable resource).

What's the problem with asset repositioning in this example? I assumed the example client earned $95,000 a year. The number one factor used to determine if a child will receive financial aid is the parent's income. In this example, it doesn't matter how many assets are repositioned from countable to non-countable assets. Because the income is too high, the child is probably not going to qualify for aid.

**Part two of Platform #2 revolves around using cash value life insurance as a savings tool for college planning.**

I went to a life insurance symposium where several insurance companies stood up in front of dozens of life insurance agents with the chore of presenting a new sales idea that could be used to sell cash value life insurance.

Several of the insurance company representatives chose to put on presentations showing why cash value life insurance is such a great savings tool for college education.

Granted, this was right after the stock market crashed 59% between 2007-2008 which caused many investors to wonder if using a 529 college savings plan was really the right way to go (most money invested in 529 plans are in mutual funds and are subject to loss when the stock market crashes).

While most readers with children or grandchildren will know what a 529 college savings plan is, let me briefly explain the advantages for those who don't.

A 529 plan is a tool that is funded after-tax (no way to fund them in a tax-deductible manner) where the money is allowed to grow tax-free and can be removed tax-free for college expenses.

Parents, grandparents, or others can gift up to $13,000 a year into a 529 plan per person without incurring a gift tax or without using part of the lifetime gift tax exemption. Contributors are allowed to supercharge 529 plans with $65,000 (5 x $13,000) per contributor in year one without gift tax issues (although no further contributions will then be allowed until year six (unless gift taxes are paid or some of the exemption is used)).

If money can grow tax-free and be removed tax-free, why would someone need to use cash value life insurance as a college savings tool?

Let me give you the sales pitch for using cash value life insurance for college planning.

1) Life insurance is a "self-completing" plan (if the breadwinner dies before fully funding for a child's education, the death benefit will "complete" that funding).

2) Money in a properly designed Equity Indexed Universal Life insurance policy grows tax-free, generates returns that are market linked, and protects the cash in the policy from stock market crashes because money can never go backwards in the policy due to negative returns (plus annual gains are locked in every year).

3) If the child does NOT go to college, the life policy will be a terrific tax-favorable/wealth-building retirement tool for the parent(s). (Money that comes out of the 529 plan will be fully income taxable if not used for college education and must be used by the age of 30).

4) After removing money from the policy for college funding for a child, it will still have cash in it and should grow for years to come (meaning that more money can be removed tax-free later on when the parent(s) is/are in retirement).

5) Money in a cash value life insurance policy is not a countable asset when a child goes to apply for financial aid for college.

Wow, after I re-read the list myself, it sure sounds like cash value life insurance is a no brainer to use for college funding, right?

Wrong.

If you run "realistic returns" in a life insurance policy and you fund it with ONLY money allocated to saving for college, it doesn't work. Barring a significant market crash right before a child takes money out of a 529 plan to pay for college (which can be mitigated by moving the money to fixed investments a few years prior to a child going to college), using a 529 plan for college savings is a better tool than cash value life insurance.

If that's the case, how can college planners sell cash value life insurance as a great college-savings tool?

Without getting into too much detail, the answer is because they manipulate the illustrative software to put forth the best of all possible scenarios when growing wealth in and, ultimately, removing money from the life insurance policy for college expenses.

For purposes of this book, I want you to take me at my word that using cash value life insurance as a college funding vehicle doesn't work. If you'd like the detail behind my conclusion, please go to www.badadvisors.com where you can download a ten-page summary wherein I explain specifically why cash value life doesn't work for college planning.

**Is there ever a time when cash value life insurance can work to save for college?**

Sure. If the parent funding the policy not only funds it for college savings but also for his/her own retirement planning.

For example, a parent might normally contribute $5,000 a year to save for a child's college expenses. If only $5,000 is paid as a premium to a cash value life insurance policy, there is no doubt that this will NOT work out well from a financial standpoint for college planning.

However, if the parent can increase the premium into the policy to $15,000 or even $25,000 a year, then a cash value policy can work very well as both a college funding vehicle and as a supplemental retirement vehicle for the parent(s).

## HOW TO DETERMINE IF A COLLEGE PLANNER IS A "BAD ADVISOR"

It's pretty simple. If you have a decent amount of assets and income over $75,000-$90,000 and you have an advisor pitch you their services for a fee because they can magically get your children qualified for financial aid, the chances are that you are dealing with a "bad advisor."

If you make more than $75,000-$90,000 and you have a college planner recommend that you reposition several of your assets into life insurance simply to qualify for aid, the chances are that you are dealing with a "bad advisor."

If you have a college planner suggest that you fund only the money you can afford to put aside for college planning into a cash value life insurance policy, the chances are that you are dealing with a "bad advisor."

## THE INFINITE BANKING SYSTEM®(IBC) OR BANK ON YOURSELF (BOY) SALES PLATFORM

Before I explain what the IBC and BOY concepts are and why I think many advisors who use these strategies are "bad advisors," I want to tell readers that the concepts are substantially similar in what they do for clients.

The IBC concept was the first one to market many years ago. Then BOY was created after the fact to compete with the IBC. Again, both concepts are basically the same.

### What is the IBC?

In their own words....

***"What if you could*** *recover the interest expenses you pay to finance cars or other major purchases?*

***What if you could*** *recover the "lost fortune" on the money you needlessly give to financial institutions?*

*What if you could do this on a tax-free basis?*

*If your answer is yes, then would you?*

*You can, if you learn how to* <u>*Become Your Own Banker*</u>*.*

*The Infinite Banking Concept will teach you how to become your own banker by:*

*Creating your own banking system using dividend-paying, permanent life insurance.*

*Using available savings and cash flow to build your own "bank."*

*Capitalizing and establishing your plan.*

*Using the method to finance your automobile purchases and even to finance your home.*

*Expanding your system to accommodate all income through a system of banks to increase your personal wealth.*

*How a business can use the concept for "equipment financing."*

## What is BOY?

In their own words....

*"It's a time-tested financial concept and tool that lets you grow your money safely and predictably, even when stocks, real estate and other investments tumble.*

*The Bank On Yourself concept uses a whole life insurance policy with some little-known features added on to it that can beat the pants off your traditional financial and retirement planning strategies.*

*Yes, we said whole life insurance... but not the kind most financial advisors and experts talk about. And we'll show you the difference in a moment.*

*Blindly following the advice of Wall Street and financial "gurus" such as Dave Ramsey and Suze Orman got you where you are. Are you happy with the state of your finances? Do you still believe their fairytale, "Buy Term (insurance) and Invest the Difference"?*

*The simple truth is that millions of Americans are hurting. They've lost 30 to 50% or more of the hard-earned savings they hoped would carry them through their retirement years in well-deserved comfort and security. Now, they may have to work for the rest of their lives just to make ends meet.*

*Bank on Yourself is the best way to invest money, if your goal is to safely grow and protect your hard-earned money and have a secure retirement you can predict and count on."*

### SOUNDS GREAT; WHERE DO I SIGN UP?

I crack myself up when I pull back the veil of marketing programs like this one. When I read the previous summaries of the IBC and BOY, I have to remind myself that I've run the math on both concepts and have come to the conclusion that neither are concepts I would recommend as wealth-building tools to clients.

But, again, the marketing of each concept sounds wonderful.

### WHAT ARE THE IBC AND BOY CONCEPTS ALL ABOUT?

It's amazingly simple which is why both programs are terrific sales tools for advisors.

These concepts revolve around the idea that debt is bad, and it's better to build a sinking fund to act as your own bank.

It's the opposite of the concept of using other peoples' money to build your wealth.

I think the best way to describe how these systems work is to simply walk you through an example.

Assume the example client is a 45-year-old married teacher. His spouse is also a teacher, and they collectively make $100,000 a year. They have two children, a home worth $250,000 with $200,000 of debt, and a nice pension plan starting to build for both of them at work. They have no meaningful savings outside of $20,000 in a 529 plan for their children.

They both lease cars with car payments totaling $600 a month.

An IBC salesperson would sit down with these clients and would tell them the wonders of becoming their own bank so they can stop being a slave to debt and so they can start paying themselves interest. The salesperson would have all sorts of wonderful illustrations showing the clients how they can grow substantial wealth with the IBC concept in a protected and tax-favorable manner.

The clients will listen, and what the salesperson says will make a lot of sense. The life insurance illustrations will also look nice.

The reality is that the clients have no idea what they are looking at, but they know they like the idea of having a "systematic plan" to grow their wealth.

The clients are told to budget themselves so they can pay X amount of money into a whole life policy over the next five-to-seven years. The goal is to build up enough cash value in the policy so money can be borrowed to purchase one or even two new cars if possible.

In a married couple situation, it is prudent to buy the life policy on the spouse who earns more income. If they earn about the same, then the policy would typically be on the female spouse's life because of lower costs of insurance.

Where does this client find the money to fund the policy? If need be, the advisor will tell the clients to stop contributing to any qualified plans or IRAs; and if they need to just become better savers, that's what they are going to have to do.

Let's fast forward seven years and assume the clients moved forward to become their own bank. Assume they will borrow, let's say, $30,000 from the life policy to buy a new car. The insurance company is charging them interest on the loan taken from the policy, but the clients will service that loan by paying back to the policy payments on a monthly basis.

Without getting into too much detail in this book about loans from life insurance policies, know that the clients are essentially paying themselves back the interest on the loan from the policy. In most whole life policies, the insurance company does charge a spread on the loan payment (1% or so typically).

In theory, this is a good way to build wealth because, once the clients build their own bank in a life insurance policy, they are avoiding paying a bank 5-8% interest on car loans. If they are paying themselves interest, they are building their own wealth in the life insurance policy instead of helping banks grow their wealth.

**What's the problem with this example?**

Have you tried to obtain a car loan lately? Many companies have no interest loans and those that don't are offering loans of between 1-5%.

What the IBC and BOY advisors won't ask you is: If you could borrow money at 0%-5% interest and reposition that money in a wealth-building tool that would grow on average at 6%-8% tax-free, would you do it?

Well, would you?

Your answer should be you'd borrow as much money as someone would give you at a 0%-5% interest rate if you could grow it at 6%-8% tax-free.

If you read the book by Nelson Nash on the IBC or the information put out on BOY, they both seemed to be obsessed with the car loan example. It's not a good example to support the use of either program.

**What other kind of debt would you pay off by becoming your own bank?**

Credit card debt? Sure. It would be much better to borrow money from a life insurance policy to pay off credit card debt than to make minimum payments to a credit card company. That sounds simple enough, right?

What's the problem with the IBC or BOY to pay off credit card debt? It takes a good 5-7 years to build up money in a policy to be able to use it as your own bank.

And why would someone fund a life insurance policy with their extra cash flow when they have tens of thousands of dollars in credit card debt? Does that make any sense?

It doesn't. Prudent financial planning advice would be to aggressively pay off high interest, non-deductible credit card debt before funding a life insurance policy to grow wealth or become your own bank.

What might make sense is to take out a home equity loan to pay off the credit card debt. The interest is deductible up to $100,000 of new debt, and the interest rate will be much lower than what the credit card company charges.

**What about becoming your own banker to pay off the debt on your home?**

Does that make sense?

Again, you have the problem of paying enough into the policy over time to have enough money to borrow out money to pay off the debt. It would take forever to fund a policy that could have enough cash to ultimately pay off a home loan. And, again, the debt itself could have been paid off directly instead of funding the policy.

Also, why would you want to pay off debt on a home that should have an interest rate of less than 6% when the interest payments are deductible (yielding an effective interest rate of 3-4% for many people).

**What other kind of debt is there that you would pay off using the IBC or BOY?**

The best I can come up with is some future debt that you don't know about yet. So you fund the life policy with your excess money and then wait to figure out later what debt you could borrow from your policy instead of from a third-party lender.

Ok. That might make some sense as long as the future debt isn't a low-interest debt or deductible (because if it is, it's better to leave the cash growing inside the life policy where it does so tax-free).

Where has this discussion led us to? It's really led us to the question: Is it a good idea to fund a cash value life insurance policy to grow wealth?

The answer is that growing wealth in a cash value life insurance policy is a terrific idea for many clients. I wrote a book, Retiring Without Risk (www.retiringwithoutrisk.com), where I explain why you should consider growing wealth with cash value life insurance (money can grow at market rates tax-free and can be removed tax-free in retirement).

## TYPES OF LIFE INSURANCE POLICIES

Let me restate the quote I found about BOY:

*The Bank On Yourself concept uses a <u>whole life insurance</u> policy with some little-known features added on to it that can beat the pants off your traditional financial and retirement planning strategies.*

Both the IBC and BOY are founded on the principals of using whole life insurance as a wealth-building tool.

Is that a good idea?

It's better than not saving for retirement; but mathematically and using historical back testing and real-world forward testing, whole life is NOT the policy people should be using to grow their wealth (in an IBC, BOY plan, or simply funding one with extra cash with no intention of becoming your own banker).

This is one of the main issues that makes a BOY or IBC advisor a "bad advisor." They seemingly are brainwashed into recommending whole life to all of their clients.

If these "bad advisors" did the research they should on the available policies in the marketplace, they would come to the conclusion that the best wealth-building life insurance policy is an Equity Indexed Universal Life (EIUL) insurance policy.

I've talked with dozens of IBC/BOY Kool-Aid drinkers, and I've never talked with one who uses EIUL for concepts they are selling.

The vast majority of the advisors I've talked with don't even know what an EIUL policy is.

This may shock you and it may not; but the ones who know about EIUL policies have told me that they understand they could recommend these policies to their clients, but the illustration software for EIUL policies is not set up to run IBC/BOY illustrations.

Do you believe that? Can you imagine the dialogue I've had about this?

Advisor: Yes, Roccy, I know I could use EIUL when helping clients implement the IBC concept.

Roccy: Then why don't you?

Advisor: Because the illustrative software at companies that offer EIUL policies is not compatible with running IBC illustrations. It's a real pain in the neck to illustrate the IBC concept with an EIUL policy, so I just use whole life instead.

Roccy: Are you kidding me? You are offering your clients an inferior product because you are having trouble illustrating it?

Advisor: Well, I'm just used to illustrating whole life and that's what I do.

Roccy: Of course.

If you think I'm making this stuff up, I'm not. You can't make this stuff up. It's unthinkable and unbelievable that an advisor would recommend an inferior insurance product simply because it's easier to illustrate. But I am dead serious when I tell you I've had this exact conversation with several IBC/BOY advisors.

## WHAT WOULD I RECOMMEND INSTEAD OF THE IBC/BOY CONCEPT?

It's not rocket science. I simply recommend that people budget themselves so they can take X amount of dollars each year to fund a good cash value life insurance policy for wealth-building/retirement-planning purposes.

I do NOT recommend borrowing from the policy in years 5, 7, 10, 15 unless you need the money in an emergency situation.

One of the only places available for people today where money can grow tax-free and be removed tax-free is a cash value life insurance policy.

Why would I want to take money out of that policy so I can forego a 0%-5% loan on a car? I wouldn't and it's not financially wise to do so.

### IS THE IBC/BOY CONCEPT BAD?

Yes and no. Is using the IBC/BOY concept better than doing nothing?

Absolutely.

Any kind of savings program is better than doing nothing.

However, systematically borrowing from a life insurance policy to pay off low interest or deductible debt is NOT a good or financially sound decision.

### WHY DO ADVISORS USE THE IBC/BOY MARKETING PLATFORM?

Because clients like systematic programs to grow wealth. The IBC/BOY sales platform has proved to work to help advisors sell millions of dollars in life insurance going back nearly 20 years.

Insurance agents only make money when they sell products. Once they find a sales track that can motivate clients to buy, they stick with it.

Therefore, the not-so-politically-correct answer as to why insurance agents use the IBC/BOY sales platform is because they can make a lot of money selling life insurance if they use it.

Does it matter that they are NOT recommending the best type of life insurance possible? To many of them it doesn't and to most of them they simply don't know any better.

Does it matter that it's better to leave the money in the policy to continue to grow tax-free rather than borrowing it out to pay off low interest or what could be deductible interest?

It would to clients if they knew any better. However, they don't and most agents selling the IBC/BOY concept don't understand the math of what they are selling and why paying off such debt with money from a life insurance policy is not the best way to build wealth.

### IBC/BOY ADVISORS: GOOD OR BAD?

Unless the advisor offers his/her clients an EIUL policy as an alternative to a whole life policy, the advisor is a "bad advisor."

If the IBC/BOY advisor doesn't understand the math behind the concept and why it is better to leave the money in the policy vs. taking it out of the policy, the advisor is a "bad advisor."

## OTHER SALES/MARKETING PLATFORMS

There are dozens of sales and marketing platforms/systems in the financial services and insurance industries.

The goal of all such platforms/systems is to motivate clients to buy whatever it is the advisors want to sell.

Most sales platforms/systems have multiple flaws to them including the main flaw which is at the heart of each program that the goal is not to provide the best advice but instead to sell as much as you can (many times with no regard to the client's best interest).

If you run across a sales platform that someone is pitching you and wonder if it has any validity to it, please feel free to e-mail me at roccy@badadvisors.com. Chances are I'm familiar with the platform, and I can tell you its pros and cons.

You can also go to www.badadvisors.com where I will have on the website a posting of various sales platforms you might want to avoid.

### CONCLUSION ON SALES - MARKETING PLATFORMS/SYSTEMS

As I've explained in this chapter, I am NOT a fan of sales/marketing systems. They are NOT client-focused, and they are NOT about giving individual custom advice to clients.

Most of them are about selling as much product as possible regardless of the client's best interest.

In fact, many of the platforms are designed to sell products to people who shouldn't be buying them. Many of the marketing systems, however, are so slick advisors are able to make sales to clients who have no business buying.

# <u>Chapter 8</u>
## Attorneys

I could write an entire book on bad advice given by attorneys. It would be very entertaining and depressing all at the same time.

What makes an attorney a "bad advisor?"

The laundry list is long. However, this book was written to give detailed information about why insurance and securities licensed advisors are "bad advisors" and fairly cursory information explaining what makes an attorney or CPA/EA/accountant a "bad advisor." This chapter will list several items you'll want to watch out for to determine if you might be dealing with an attorney who is a "bad advisor."

### CLASSIC ATTORNEY WORK

Why do most people go to an attorney?

Most do so to obtain a will, living trust, durable power of attorney, etc.

Why have a will? So you can dictate who will get your money/assets upon death and to direct who will receive custody of your children (if you have children under 18) in the event or your untimely death.

Why have Durable Powers (legal and medical)? Legal powers allow someone to legally act on your behalf in the event you become incapacitated. Medical powers allow an appointed person to make life-sustaining medical decisions for you in the event you become incapacitated (like removing or not a feeding tube to sustain life).

Why have living trusts (also known as marital trusts or A&B trusts if married)? These are used to minimize estate taxes paid upon death and to avoid what can be a very costly and time-consuming probate process.

People who own or run a business also go to attorneys to receive advice on corporate structure and other business advice.

## LACK OF FOLLOW THROUGH WITH ESTATE-PLANNING DOCUMENTS

One classic mistake or omission many estate-planning attorneys make is that they do not finish the job many times when it comes to estate-planning documents.

It's one thing to charge a client $2,500+ for wills, trusts, and durable powers. It's another to charge that much money for documents and then not follow through with the process to make sure the client's assets are owned in such a manner so that the documents are used to their fullest benefit.

What am I talking about? In most states, if your assets are not owned by your trust (titled in the trust's name), they will still pass through the probate process. Why is this a bad thing? Because the probate process can be very expensive, time consuming, and provides no privacy.

Let's go over a quick and simple example to show you what many times happens when an estate plan is not completed and the potential consequences.

Mr. and Mrs. Smith have their wills, durable powers, and marital trusts drafted by attorney Green. The Smiths just left attorney Green's office with their signed/executed documents.

They feel good about the fact that they finally took the time to get their estate plan in order.

What's the problem? Assume that the Smiths have $2,000,000 worth of assets titled currently in their own names. If the Smiths die in an auto accident shortly after signing their documents, all of the assets NOT owned by their marital trusts WILL pass through probate.

So what? Assume the Smiths live in Cook County, Illinois. The average probate fees on assets that are probated are approximately 10%. That means the children will have $200,000 less in assets because their parents' lawyer did not follow through with the estate-planning process.

Part of the process when having your estate plan done by an attorney is making sure you re-title all of your assets in the name of your living trust(s). They are revocable trusts. Therefore, it's like you still own the assets individually (meaning you have access to them); except, at death, the assets will avoid probate (and the expenses and headaches that go along with such a process).

What kind of attorney is a "bad advisor?" One who takes your money to create estate-planning documents and then doesn't finish the job.

## ATTORNEYS MAKE YOU THINK THEY KNOW MORE THAN THEY ACTUALLY DO!

This may not come as a complete surprise to most readers, but attorneys don't know half as much as they want you to think they do.

The joke among us attorneys is that, when we get a question from a client or potential client that we don't know the answer to, we say: *"That's a very good question. Let me research that, and I'll have an answer for you next time we meet."*

That allows the attorney who doesn't know a subject matter or a question to bill the client for the time to research it. It's a bit comical that clients will pay thousands of dollars to an attorney to research many topics that they really should already know. The attorney is making himself/herself more knowledgeable and more valuable to the next and all future clients, and the current client is paying him/her for this.

## WHAT KIND OF ADVICE SHOULD YOU NOT EXPECT TO RECEIVE FROM AN ATTORNEY?

Comprehensive estate-planning is the biggest one to watch out for. While I just outlined a classic estate-planning blunder many attorneys fall prey to, that example does not speak to the limited knowledge and ability of most attorneys when it comes to comprehensive estate-planning.

Here is a classic definition of estate-planning: It is the process of anticipating and arranging for the disposal of an estate. Estate-planning typically attempts to eliminate uncertainties over the administration of a probate and maximize the value of the estate by reducing taxes and other expenses. Guardians are often designated for minor children and incapacitated beneficiaries.

When a client goes to an attorney and pays $2,500 or more for estate-planning advice, there is an expectation that the client will receive "real" estate-planning advice. Unfortunately, many times that is not the case.

What's my definition of "comprehensive" estate-planning advice? It would be advice from an attorney who knows the following:

- -wills
- -trusts
- -durable powers
- -irrevocable trusts
    - -life insurance
    - -dynasty
    - -international
- -estate tax mitigation/avoidance
    - -defective trusts
    - -family limited partnerships
    - -freeze partnerships
    - -GRATs, GRUTs, etc.
    - -charitable planning
        - -CRTs, CLTs, family foundations, etc.
    - -captive insurance companies
    - -installment note structures
- -asset protection
    - -domestic
    - -international
- -long-term care insurance
- -life insurance
    - -premium finance
    - -no cash value permanent policies
- -annuities
- -income planning
- -disability insurance
- -life settlements
- -reverse mortgages
- -Medicaid planning

The previous list is not an exhaustive one; but it should get my point across that there is a lot to know if an attorney is going to give truly comprehensive estate-planning advice.

**Who really needs "comprehensive" estate planning advice?**

People with an estate net worth over $5,000,000 and $10,000,000 would be even better.

Does that mean if you do not have an estate net worth of $5,000,000 or more you can receive adequate estate-planning advice from a "bad advisor" attorney who barely knows the basics?

No. If you have a net worth of $1,000,000 or more, you really deserve to deal with an attorney who knows more than just wills, trusts, and durable powers.

In fact, if you have an estate of less than $1,000,000, it is imperative to work with an attorney who knows proper Medicaid planning techniques.

### EXAMPLES OF BAD ADVICE

Again, this chapter could be an entire book. I could go through examples for the next 50+ pages illustrating why attorneys who do not know all of the items on the previous list could give bad advice to certain clients. Instead of doing that, I'm going to pick two example clients to demonstrate what makes an attorney a "bad advisor."

### SENIOR CLIENT WITH LESS THAN $1,000,000 IN ASSETS

Here is the fact pattern. The client is a 75-year-old single lady who is in declining health. She has a net worth of $650,000 ($100,000 in an IRA, $100,000 in CDs, and a $200,000 home with no debt). She has three children and five grandchildren. She has a paid-up $250,000 life insurance policy.

She receives $1,500 a month in gross retirement income from a pension and Social Security payments.

She wants an estate plan that will protect her assets from the government, long-term care expenses, and pass the maximum amount of wealth to her heirs at death.

She goes to the local estate-planning attorney and guess what documents he sets her up with?

1) will
2) durable powers
3) revocable living trusts

He charged her $2,500 for the documents. She came in and signed them, walked out with a copy, and then she never had any more interaction with the attorney.

**What if she dies within a short period of time after signing the documents?**

How did the estate-planning advice turn out?

The will poured over assets into the trust, and they were distributed per her wishes. Sounds good, right?

What about probate?

The attorney did not counsel or help the client transfer all of the appropriate assets to the trust so they all (except the life insurance proceeds) passed through the probate process at a cost of 7% of the total assets to the estate ($28,000).

This is classic advice from an attorney I would deem a "bad advisor." He should have made sure that the client changed the title to her property to the living trust to make sure the assets would not pass through the probate process.

**What if the client ends up in a nursing home in the near or even distant future?**

Many clients think that <u>Medicaid</u> will step in to pay for their nursing home care. That is NOT the case. This client has $198,000 of "countable" assets ($100,000 in CDs and $100,000 in the IRA).

What the attorney and the client don't know is that that she will have to spend down her "countable" assets to $2,000 before being able to qualify for financial assistance from Medicaid.

The attorney was hired to help the client with estate planning. That includes helping mitigate expenses of the estate and passing the maximum amount of wealth to her heirs.

What advice should have been given?

1) The client should have been made aware of the issues with Medicaid spend-down rules that would require the client to spend down her assets to $2,000 prior to being able to qualify for Medicaid.

2) She should have been made aware that any gifts made within five years of her attempt to qualify for Medicaid will cause a penalty period that will delay her ability to receive financial aid.

3) She should have been told to consider funding a funeral trust to pay for her funeral expenses. Such an expense is an exempt expenditure for Medicaid gift purposes and won't count against her.

4) She should have been told about a gifting program to start the five-year lookback clock running on such gifts so when she is ready to qualify for Medicaid she can.

5) The attorney should have discussed the pros and cons of buying long-term care insurance to protect the client from the devastating costs of nursing home care. This could be a traditional policy or a single premium life insurance policy with a long-term care benefit.

6) The attorney should have explained to the client what a life settlement is and whether one would make sense with her life insurance policy (it probably won't, but it should have been brought up for discussion).

7) The attorney should have discussed what to do with the client's personal residence. The home will be used to pay back any benefits provided to the client through Medicaid. It might be prudent to use a Qualified Personal Residence Trust (QPRT) to gift the house out of the estate and allow her to live in it for a period of years.

8) Additionally, a reverse mortgage might be prudent to the extent the client wants to increase cash flow (probably not, but it is something that should have been discussed).

And the list goes on....

The point with this example isn't to have me explain in detail Medicaid planning, life settlements, reverse mortgages, etc. To do so would take 20+ pages and is not the point of this book.

The point of this book is to point out when advisors are "bad advisors" and an attorney who gives estate-planning advice to a client who has a net worth of less than $1,000,000 who does NOT understand proper Medicaid planning techniques is a "bad advisor."

If you wanted me to guess how many estate-planning attorneys know how to give compliant Medicaid planning advice, I'd put the number at less than 10% (meaning there is a lot of bad advice being given in the legal community today).

## 60-YEAR OLD CLIENT WHO IS WORTH $10 MILLION DOLLARS

Let's now look at an example client who is the opposite of a client who is a candidate for Medicaid planning.

Assume the following facts: Mr. Smith is 60-years old and runs a small but profitable company (treated as a C-Corporation for tax purposes) that is worth $5,000,000. He earns $250,000 annually (pre-tax), and his goal in five years is to pass the business to his son who also works for the company. He is married and has three children and three grandchildren.

He has $1,000,000 in a qualified retirement plan and aggressively funds the maximum amount tax-deferred into the plan every year. He has a $500,000 house with no debt. He has two rental properties that he owns in his own name. He owns in his own name the building his company works from. He has a $2,000,000 brokerage account.

His estate-planning goals are to pass the business to his children without gift taxes or estate taxes, minimize estate taxes on the entire estate, reduce or eliminate probate costs, protect his estate from long-term care costs, and make sure he never runs out of money in retirement.

The amount of concepts that need to be considered and the advice that needs to be given to this client are significant. In the following material, I will list the concepts/tools that need to be considered with a brief explanation next to some of them. Again, my goal is not to make you an expert in the concepts/tools discussed (which would take ten or more pages), I am simply trying to impress upon you how much an attorney who I would consider a "good advisor" needs to know and discuss with clients who have wealth.

-wills, trusts, and durable powers.

-long-term care insurance purchased through the C-Corporation in a 100% tax-deductible manner and in a discriminatory manner.

-intentionally defective grantor trust sale to transition the company to the next generation in a gift and estate tax-favorable manner (this structure involves placing the company in a discounted family limited partnership to increase the leverage of the sale).

-LLC #1 for rental property #1 for asset protection and for potential use in a leveraged gifting program or sale to a defective trust.

-LLC #2 for rental property #2 (same reason as for LLC #1).

-LLC #3 for the commercial building (same reason as for LLC #1).

-family limited partnership for the brokerage account for asset protection and for potential use in a leveraged gifting program or sale to a defective trust.

-international LLC for the brokerage account (serves the same purpose as a domestic LLC or FLP except it provides better asset protection).

-an Offshore Asset Protection Trust (OAPT) for the brokerage account (an OAPT provides the best asset protection available and can have dynastic benefits similar for estate-planning).

-an Irrevocable Life Insurance Trust (ILIT) where life insurance (probably a $2^{nd}$ to die policy) can be purchased and where the death benefit will pass to the heirs without income or estate taxes. Life insurance could also be purchased in the defective trust.

-reverse mortgage to leverage the home and to buy a large life insurance policy in an ILIT to maximize the amount of assets passed to the heirs.

-the attorney should counsel the client to immediately stop funding his tax-deferred qualified plan. The money in the qualified plan is likely to be double taxed (income and estate taxes) at the client's death, and it is the worst asset in the client's entire estate.

-an 831(b) Captive Insurance Company (CIC) could be an invaluable tool to both insure uninsured risks of his company and also shift sizable amounts of tax-deductible premiums to his heirs. The CIC could be owned by an irrevocable trust for the benefit of the heirs. A CIC could also be used to shift some of the value of the company to the CIC which would help when trying to transition the company to the next generation with minimum gift and estate taxes.

-a guaranteed income for life annuity should be discussed to help secure for the client a lifetime income. Once an appropriate guaranteed lifetime income is secured, it frees up the client to start an aggressive gift-giving program of other assets without fear that the client will run out of money in retirement because of the gifts.

There are actually several other tools/concepts I could list that should be discussed with this example client, but the list I have should get my point across.

What point? That attorneys, in order to not be deemed "bad advisors," have to know a lot about a lot in order to provide more affluent clients comprehensive estate-planning advice.

How many attorneys giving estate-planning advice know what they need to know in order to give comprehensive advice to affluent clients?

Less than 5% (which means there are a lot of "bad advisors" out there giving legal advice to clients who don't know any better).

## SUMMARY ON DETERMINING IF AN ATTORNEY IS A "BAD ADVISOR"

Most attorneys who give estate-planning advice are average or below average. They can help you with wills, trusts, durable powers, and an irrevocable life insurance trust.

Some will take the time to make sure your living trusts are funded so your assets don't have to pass through the probate process.

However, many of the attorneys giving estate planning advice I would consider "bad advisors."

Why?

Because most attorneys giving advice to clients who have a net worth of less than $1,000,000 know nothing or very little about Medicaid planning. In my opinion, it is nearly impossible to give advice to a client 60 or older if the attorney doesn't know the somewhat complex rules that govern clients receiving financial aid from Medicaid.

Practically speaking, if you are younger and have few assets, you could go to virtually any attorney and receive adequate estate-planning advice. The main reason is because such clients don't require much (just a simple will, living trust(s), and durable powers of attorney).

If you are someone with a larger estate, you definitely need to work with an attorney who is not just going to be discussing wills, trusts, and durable powers. You will want an attorney who knows all of the topics/concepts I listed earlier in this chapter.

The consequences of using an attorney who is a "bad advisor" or one who is maybe not a "bad advisor" but one who is just not as good as you could find can be financially significant (meaning it can cost you and/or your heirs millions of dollars).

## QUESTIONS TO ASK ATTORNEYS TO DETERMINE IF THEY ARE "BAD ADVISORS"

These questions are fairly simple.

1) Do you have a pattern and practice of following up with your clients to make sure that, after documents are signed, everything that needs to get done after the fact to maximize the use of the documents gets done?

2) If you are 60 or older and have an estate of less than $1,000,000, you must ask your attorney if he/she is familiar with the Medicaid qualification rules and if he/she incorporates Medicaid planning into estate-planning advice.

3) If you have a net worth of $5,000,000 or more, you need to ask your attorney if he/she is familiar with all of the following: - wills, trusts, durable powers, irrevocable trusts, life insurance, dynasty trusts, international trusts, defective trusts, family limited partnerships, freeze partnerships, GRATs, GRUTs, CRTs, CLTs, family foundations, captive insurance companies, installment note structures, asset protection (domestic and international), long-term care insurance, life insurance (premium finance, no cash value permanent policies), annuities, life settlements, reverse mortgages, etc.

If the attorney is not familiar with the items above, you need to find an attorney who is. Again, using an attorney who doesn't know all of the advanced-planning tools (and business transition if you are a business owner) can cost you and/or your heirs millions of dollars at your death.

# Chapter 9
## CPAs/EAs/Accountants

Most CPAs/EAs/accountants (hereinafter CPAs) stick to classic accounting work. However, some have ventured off into financial services, life insurance, annuities, etc.

The main purpose of this chapter is to let you know some of the limitations of most CPAs when it comes to the out-of-the box advice some are offering/providing.

I will also briefly discuss why most CPAs do not offer "advanced" tax-planning advice.

### CLASSIC ACCOUNTING WORK

Why do most people go to a CPA?

It depends on who you are.

If you are an individual who works for someone else (you are a W-2 employee), you probably go to a CPA simply to have your annual income taxes done.

If you own or run a small business, your CPA will typically help you with any one of a number of items:

-Annual corporate tax returns
-Payroll and 941 payments
-Quarterly reports
-Profit and loss as well as other financial statements
-Bill payments

Unfortunately, I don't know of any way to help you determine if the CPA providing the above services is a "good" or "bad advisor."

You'll find this out if and when you or your business is audited.

## DO CPAs PROVIDE "REAL" TAX-PLANNING?

The title begs the question: What is "real" tax-planning?

Let me give you my definition of "real" tax-planning.

"Real" tax planning isn't simply taking a client's financial information, putting it into a calculator, and telling them how much in taxes they owe.

"Real" tax planning is proactive tax-planning. It's when a CPA looks at a client's situation (business or personal) and tries to use every bit of the tax code to their advantage to reduce taxes.

What kind of taxes am I talking about mitigating or avoiding? All types (income, capital gains, estate, and gift).

### Business owner example—

Assume Dr. Smith is an orthopedic surgeon whose medical practice grosses $1.5 million a year. Assume Dr. Smith has four employees; and after all the overhead and other expenses are paid, assume his pre-tax, take-home pay is $750,000 a year.

Assume Dr. Smith is 45-years old, is married, and has three children. Assume he has minimal debt except his home loan and that his goals are to minimize income taxes and grow a secure retirement nest egg.

What advice is he typically going to receive from his CPA? For the most part, a CPA will take his financial data from the business and his personal data, apply the typical business and personal deductions, and then tell Dr. Smith what he owes the IRS each year.

### Is Dr. Smith's CPA a "bad advisor?"

It depends. It depends on the expectations Dr. Smith has of his CPA.

If the CPA sets Dr. Smith's expectation at the outset of the relationship that he would only be "processing" tax returns vs. giving proactive tax-planning advice, then I would not consider the CPA a "bad advisor." (Although the CPA would certainly not be one I would want to hire or would recommend to clients).

If the CPA touted himself as someone who knows how to help clients reduce their taxes, then I would consider him a "bad advisor."

Why?

Because no proactive tax-planning advice was given.

How could this example CPA have helped Dr. Smith reduce his income taxes?

The main way would have been through the use of a tax-deferred, qualified-retirement plan. To give competent advice on tax-deferred qualified plans, the CPA would need to be familiar with 401(k) plans, profit sharing plans, defined benefit plans, 412(e)(3) defined benefit plans, cash balance plans, and 401(h) plans.

CPAs should also know the pitfalls and limitations to SEP and SIMPLE IRAs (which should never be recommended; a discussion of which is outside the scope of this material).

You know how many CPAs I've met in my life who know the ins and outs of all of the above-mentioned plans? ZERO.

I've met many who know something about 401(k) plans and profit sharing plans.

I've met some who know defined benefit plans.

I've met a smaller few who know anything about cash balance plans.

And I've met none who are familiar with 401(h) plans.

If you are curious, a 401(h) plan is one that is funded in a tax-deductible manner where the money can grow tax-free and be removed tax-free for medical expenses (medical expenses are a certainty for every retiree at some point in their lives).

With a properly designed 401(k)/profit sharing plan/cash balance/401(h) plan, it is likely that Dr. Smith could income tax defer $150,000 or more for retirement through the business (saving him nearly half that much in annual taxes).

**Let me take it one step further**. Not only should the CPA know the previously mentioned plans; but he/she should also be familiar with IRAs, Roth IRAs, and even Roth 401(k) plans.

While most successful small business owners cannot deduct payments to a traditional IRA or even fund a Roth IRA (because of income limits), they can fund a Roth 401(k) plan.

While Roth IRAs and 401(k) plans are funded with after-tax dollars, once funded, the money can grow without taxes and be removed without taxes in retirement. I'm not going to go through the math, but most clients can grow more wealth using Roth IRAs or Roth 401(k) plans vs. the tax-deductible version of either.

**Let me take it one step further**. If a CPA is going to give proactive income tax planning advice to a 45-year old, he/she better understand the math behind using cash value life insurance as a tax-favorable/wealth-building tool.

Why?

Because as I explain in great detail in my book, <u>Retiring Without Risk</u> and as I've alluded to several times in earlier chapters, for many clients under the age of 55, growing wealth with a properly designed cash value life insurance policy can be more advantageous than IRAs, Roth IRAs, Roth 401(k) plans, profit sharing plans, defined benefit plans, 412(e)(3) defined benefit plans, or cash balance plans.

While the previous material may sound a little comical, my point is to illustrate that, even though CPAs who tout that they know how to give income tax planning advice to clients because they know 401(k) plans, profit sharing plans, and defined benefit plans, they can still be categorized as "bad advisors" because they don't know the alternative wealth-building tools.

**Let me take it one step further**. If a CPA is going to give proactive income tax-planning advice, he/she should know the proper use of Captive Insurance Companies (CICs).

CICs can be one of the most, if not the most, powerful tax-planning/wealth-building tools available to business owners. CICs can also be tremendous tools to mitigate or avoid gift taxes and estate taxes.

I won't go into a detailed discussion about CICs because this book is not supposed to educate readers on the details of tax-planning/wealth-building tools; but know that, if you had a room full of 100 CPAs, you could count on one hand the number who knew anything about CICs.

**Let me take it one step further**. Actually, for the sake of brevity, I'm not going to take it a step further. Instead, I'll point you to Chapter 10 where you can read a list of concepts/products/tools that various advisors should be familiar with in order to give comprehensive advice to their clients (like being able to take a 100% deduction for long-term care insurance if the company is properly structured). You can use that list to probe the knowledge of your advisors (including your CPA) to determine if they are "bad advisors."

## WHAT ABOUT CORPORATE STUCTURE ADVICE?

If you own or run a small business or are thinking of starting one, it would make logical sense that you would ask your CPA for help in determining what type of entity should be used, right? Wrong.

The number one failure I see with CPAs is the advice given when it comes to corporate structure.

Many CPAs have their small business clients set up as sole proprietors instead of S-Corporations, C-Corporations, or Limited Liability Companies (LLCs).

Why?

Because sole proprietorships are cheap to form and run every year (no corporate filings, etc.).

However, sole proprietorships provide NO asset protection and should **NEVER be used**.

Because CPAs for some reason focus in on the cost of structures vs. the benefits of them, many sole proprietorships are formed every year at their recommendation.

Besides asset protection, there are tax reasons to be an S-Corporation or C-Corporation (or what would be better is an LLC treated as a C-Corporation or S-Corporation for tax purposes).

My point, to keep this section brief, is that if you're looking for advice about what corporate structure should be used for a business and if your CPA doesn't have specific reasons for recommending an S-Corporation, C-Corporation, or a Limited Liability Company (LLC), you are working with a "bad advisor." If the CPA recommends a sole proprietorship, you are also working with a "bad advisor."

### FINANCIAL PLANNING SERVICES

If your CPA has not started offering financial services yet, just wait, it's coming.

While CPAs have been slow to embrace their ability to give advice to clients on financial planning services, the momentum is picking up.

When I say financial services, what do I mean?

I mean that CPAs have been allowed for years to give investment advice or sell stocks, mutual funds, bonds, variable annuities, etc., to clients. I mean that a CPA can be your financial planner or money manager now.

What do I mean when I say "now they can..."? For years, CPAs were not allowed to sell products or give investment advice to clients.

While many still do not sell products or give financial-planning advice to clients, they have been allowed to do so for many years. Allowed by whom? The AICPA (American Institute for Certified Public Accountants).

For years the AICPA forbade CPAs from offering financial-planning advice and selling products to clients. Why? Because they were concerned that CPAs would abuse their "trusted advisor" status and they wanted CPAs to avoid conflict-of-interest issues.

What conflict-of-interest issues? The conflict of a trusted advisor taking advantage of that relationship to sell products that may be in the CPA's best interest vs. the client's best interest.

## CPAs ARE THE "TRUSTED" ADVISOR

If you read any of the studies, you'll find that, out of the list of advisors we all have in our lives, CPAs are considered the most trusted. Think about the following list: Who do you trust most to give you an unbiased opinion on various tax, estate-planning, financial-planning, insurance products, etc.?

-Insurance agent
-Stockbroker
-Financial planner
-CFP®
-Attorney
-CPA/EA/accountant

CPAs are the overwhelming favorite from the previous list.

Why?

Because everyone knows that insurance agents, stock brokers, financial planners, and CFP®s are salespeople and, therefore, do not come with the trustworthiness of someone who is not a salesperson (or so that's the stereotype).

What about attorneys? They are not selling products or financial-planning advice (at least most are not because the American Bar Association does not allow it). As an attorney, I can tell you there is some amount of trust in attorneys; but as you know from watching TV, the perception of attorneys is not always that of someone who is trustworthy (actually it can be just the opposite).

Who does that leave people to trust? The CPA.

By reading this book, you are now on notice that your CPA could, in fact, be a wolf-in-sheep's clothing. Your CPA, who you trust, could also be in the financial-planning business or even in the insurance business (and that in and of itself isn't a bad thing as long as the CPA is not a "bad advisor").

## SHOULD YOU TRUST YOUR CPA TO MANAGE YOUR MONEY OR GIVE YOU FINANCIAL-PLANNING ADVICE?

First, I would suggest that you re-read the chapters on Broker Dealers, financial planners and fee-only advisors. Just because your CPA is the one offering you financial planning or investment advice, it doesn't mean that he/she is not subject to the same problems that all financial planners and stock brokers have.

Actually, aside from the select few CPAs who really learn the subject matter, most CPAs provide inferior financial-planning/wealth-building advice than the typical full-time financial planner.

Why?

Let me give you the typical profile of a CPA who offers investment advice to clients.

The CPAs are told by several colleagues that they should obtain their securities license so they can make more money. Most CPAs are reluctant to do so because they do not want to risk losing clients who pay them annually for tax work.

However, many CPAs who are making less money (due to all the clients using discounted tax services or do-it-yourself tax programs) have decided to move forward to obtain their securities licenses for the very purpose of using their trusted client database for investment services.

Do most CPAs have a real interest in learning the ins and outs of proper money management? No.

Do most of them have time to really become full-service money managers? No.

If that's the case, how do CPAs provide such services?

They work through a Broker Dealer (BD) who will step in and provide these services for their clients. In other words, the CPA is not really the one giving advice or making recommendations. The advice is coming from the BD (many of whom have special platforms for CPAs who want to offer financial-planning/money-management advice).

Is this a good idea? If you've read the chapter in this book on what's wrong with broker dealers and securities licensed advisors, you know the answer is a resounding no.

## HOW DO YOU DETERMINE IF A CPA OFFERING FINANCIAL SERVICES IS A "BAD ADVISOR?"

Again, turn to the end of the chapter on BDs and securities licensed advisors and go through those questions first. Then you should simply ask your CPA what he/she does on a daily basis to be the "best" financial planner/money manager he/she can be.

If the answer is that the CPA simply looks to a BD to give advice, then you know you are dealing with a "bad advisor."

If the CPA is a full-time financial planner/money manager who has foregone his/her full-time accounting work, then there is a chance that he/she is not a "bad advisor." These types of CPAs will be few and far between.

## WHAT ABOUT CPAs WHO SELL LIFE INSURANCE OR ANNUITIES?

It's interesting, but there are a lot fewer CPAs who sell their trusted clients life insurance and/or annuities. I think the reason is because there are tenfold as many Broker Dealers who market to CPAs vs. insurance companies or Independent Marketing Organizations (IMOs) marketing to them to sell life insurance and annuities.

When I give advice to CPAs on how to grow their business, I routinely tell them that they should be selling their clients life insurance and annuities, not securities.

Why?

Because it's nearly impossible to be a full-time CPA and a full-time financial planner/money manager. Additionally, insurance products are not nearly as volatile as stocks, mutual funds, bonds, etc. When the stock market tanks like it did from 2000-2002 (-46%) and again from 2007-2008 (-59%), no matter how wonderful of a money manager you are, your clients' money is going to go backwards (and probably a lot).

I tell CPAs they are taking a much bigger risk of losing their clients when they manage their money.

However, when dealing with certain life and annuity products, CPAs can guarantee that their clients' money will not go backward and that, when gains are achieved in certain products, they are locked in on an annual basis.

Additionally, most fixed life and annuity products today do not need much monitoring (unlike a stock portfolio that needs constant monitoring).

Think about it. If there were fixed annuities that could guarantee a rate of return of between 7-8% on an accumulation value that is coupled with a guaranteed income for life a client could never outlive, would that be more comfortable for a CPA to sell than a mutual fund that could lose 59% of its value in less than two years? I think so.

If there were cash value life insurance policies where the money could grow up to 15% a year with NO risk of loss where the money would grow tax-free and come out tax-free and where the gains were locked in every year, would offering such a product be more comfortable than stocks or mutual funds that have no protection from stock market losses? I think so.

Then, if you run into a CPA who is offering mainly insurance products, such an advisor must be considered a "good advisor" not a "bad advisor," right?

Wrong.

Please re-read the chapter of this book on IMOs and the other chapter on bad insurance advisors. Not only do CPAs have the issues discussed in those chapters; but, again, most CPAs are trying to be insurance agents on a part-time basis. Many insurance agents do a bad job when they do it on a full-time basis. While CPAs might be considered more trusted than a typical insurance agent, that's a bit of a problem when most CPAs do not have the time to become proficient in the products they are selling.

## HOW DO YOU DETERMINE IF A CPA SELLING LIFE INSURANCE OR ANNUITES IS A "BAD ADVISOR?"

Again, go to the back of the chapter on IMOs and the one on insurance agents and ask those questions first. Then simply ask your CPA if he/she is a full-time insurance agent or a part-time insurance agent. If the answer is that the CPA is a part-time insurance agent, the chances are significant that he/she is a "bad advisor."

## WHAT ABOUT ESTATE-PLANNING ADVICE?

Let me conclude this chapter with a little discussion about CPAs and estate-planning.

Most CPAs know the basics about estate-planning (that you should have a will, living trust, and durable powers of attorney).

Outside of that, it gets a bit dicey.

Estate-planning for what I'll call non-affluent clients is not terribly difficult (non-affluent being someone who is worth less than $1 million). Although anyone giving advice to clients over 65 with less than $1 million in assets should know how to give Medicaid planning advice.

It would take a separate chapter to discuss all the nuances of estate-planning and what a CPA would need to know in order to give competent advice to affluent clients.

Instead of a lengthy discussion, I'll simply list many of the estate-planning tools that a CPA would need to be familiar with in order to give competent advice. If a CPA is giving comprehensive or complex estate-planning advice to clients without being very familiar with the following, I would consider the CPA a "bad advisor."

Wills; Durable Powers of Attorney; A&B, Marital, or Living Trusts; Irrevocable Life Insurance Trusts (ILIT); Dynasty Trusts; Divorce Protection; Family Limited Partnerships; General Partnerships; Limited Partnerships; IRS Challenges; Discounting Strategies; Gifting Strategies; Freeze Partnerships; Preferred/Non-Preferred Interests; Grantor Retained Annuity Trusts; Generation-Skipping Tax-Planning Issues; Intentionally Defective Grantor Trusts; Structured Sales; Self-Canceling Installment Notes; Split

Interest Gifts; Charitable Gift Annuities; Charitable Remainder Trusts; Charitable Remainder Annuity Trust; Charitable Remainder Unitrust; Donor Advised Funds; Charitable Lead Trusts; Grantor Lead Trusts; Non-grantor Lead Trusts; Private Foundations, and Captive Insurance Companies.

The previous list is not an exhaustive list. However, if your CPA knows the items on this list, the chances of him/her knowing most of the rest of the tools needed to give comprehensive estate-planning advice is significant.

The bottom line with most CPAs and estate-planning is that you should probably not look to them for anything but the most basic advice.

### QUESTIONS TO ASK CPAs/EAs/ACCOUNTANTS TO DETERMINE IF THEY ARE "BAD ADVISORS"

The questions you ask a CPA will be determined by the type of advice they are touting that they can give you.

#### For CPAs who want to give "tax-planning" advice—

Let me preface these questions by stating that, if you only want your annual personal tax return done, it's very difficult to determine if you are working with a "bad advisor." The following questions are more geared towards readers who are more affluent or who own or run small businesses.

1) What kind of corporate entity should you use for your business?

If the CPA says a sole proprietorship is ok or a good idea, you know you are working with a "bad advisor."

2) Why should your business be a C-Corporation, S-Corporation, or LLC treated for tax purposes as either a C- or S-Corporation?

If the CPA doesn't have specific reasons why your business should be one or the other, you are dealing with a "bad advisor."

I could argue that, from an asset-protection point of view, if the CPA didn't recommend a multi-member LLC treated as either a C-Corporation or S-Corporation, you are dealing with a "bad advisor."

3) What is the best way to reduce income taxes?

This is an open-ended question, but the CPA should know the basics about: 401(k) plans, profit sharing plans, defined benefit plans, 412(e)(3) defined benefit plans, cash balance plans, and 401(h) plans, IRAs, Roth IRAs, Roth 401(k) plans, captive insurance companies, and why not to use SEP and SIMPLE IRAs.

If the CPA is giving income-tax planning advice and doesn't know the pros and cons of the previously mentioned plans, he/she is a "bad advisor."

I could also argue that, if the CPA doesn't understand the math of using cash value life insurance as a tax-favorable and protective wealth-building tool, he/she would also be considered a "bad advisor."

I could also argue that, if the CPA doesn't understand how to properly use captive insurance companies to help affluent business owners reduce taxes and build wealth, he/she would also be considered a "bad advisor."

### For CPAs who want to give "financial planning" advice—

1) Does the CPA practice full-time as a financial planner or does he/she work mainly as a CPA who outsources money management to a third party (usually through a Broker Dealer platform).

If the CPA outsources the work to a third party, the chances are significant that you are dealing with a "bad advisor." While the third party may do a decent or even good job of managing your money, the CPA is most likely a "bad advisor" because the chances he/she has any idea if the ongoing advice given to clients is any good or is in the client's best interest is slim to none.

2) Does the CPA understand Fixed Indexed Annuities (FIAs) and Equity Indexed Universal Life (EIUL). If not, you are dealing with a "bad advisor."

3) See all the questions at the end of the chapter on IMOs, financial planners, and fee-only planners.

### For CPAs who want to give advice on life insurance or annuities—

Again, go to the back of the chapter on IMOs and the one on insurance agents and ask those questions first. Then simply ask your CPA if he/she is a full-time insurance agent or a part-time insurance agent. If the answer is that the CPA is a part-time insurance agent, the chances are significant that he/she is a "bad advisor."

### For CPAs who want to give advice on "estate planning"—

If you turn back three pages, I list the topics that a CPA should know in order to give estate-planning advice.

### SUMMARY ABOUT CPAs BEING "BAD ADVISORS"

Generally speaking, CPAs/EAs/accountants are the advisor least likely to be deemed a "bad advisor."

**CPAs become "bad advisors" when they get out of their box to try to provide services they don't know much about and/or don't have a significant interest in** (besides making money selling to their trusted database of clients). Those services are usually financial-planning advice and/or money-management services.

Some CPAs venture into the life insurance and annuity business as well and most fall prey to the same problems that are outlined in the chapter on insurance agents.

The bottom line is that you need to know what you are talking about before assessing if your CPA knows what he/she is talking about. Hopefully, by using this chapter coupled with several others, you will be well armed to determine if the CPA you are working with is a "bad advisor."

# Chapter 10
## Concepts/Products
## Good Advisors Should Know

My books are all somewhat opinionated (although I back my opinions up with fact, math, the tax code, statistics, etc.).

This chapter gives you my opinion on the concepts and products "good advisors" should know. Why? So they can offer the best/most comprehensive advice to their clients.

There is no easy way to list the specific topics that each advisor should know. There are several different types of advisors who tout that they can help clients on a multiple of different levels.

For example, insurance agent number one might be very clear that he/she is only going to help you with finding the right life insurance policy to protect your family in the event you die.

Then there is insurance agent number two who is marketing his services more as a retirement planner who can show you how to grow wealth in a protected manner.

For example, securities licensed advisor number one might make it very clear that he/she is simply interested in selling you the best mutual fund that will be used as part of the growth segment of the money in your IRA.

Then there is securities licensed advisor number two who is a CFP® and who touts the ability to provide for you a comprehensive financial/estate plan.

Each advisor is setting a different expectation for the services that they can offer; and depending on what they tout they are providing, they need to know specific concepts and products.

Because there is no great way to list the concepts/products in an order that fits each individual advisor, I'm simply going to list them in sort of a hodgepodge manner. The list is fairly extensive, but it's important that readers know that there are a lot of good ideas and products out there that their trusted advisors should know.

To put in a little plug for my educational institute, I teach advisors what they need to know about the following concepts/products so they can provide the "best" and most comprehensive advice to their clients.

If you would like your advisors to learn about the education provided through The Wealth Preservation Institute, simply have them go to www.thewpi.org.

In the following list of concepts/products, I sometimes give a paragraph or more explanation of what they are and how they can be beneficial. With others, I've simply taken excerpts of bullet points from the CWPP™, CAPP™, or CMP™ course outlines.

Again, keep in mind that I'm not trying to fully explain each concept/product. I'm simply illustrating the vastness of what's out there in an effort to allow you to learn a little about the concepts/products so you can determine if you think your current or future advisors should know a few or many of them before you hire or work with them.

One thing you'll notice absent from this chapter is a list of investments "good advisors" should know about. The goal of this book is not to tell you how to identify if your stockbroker or money manager knows what he/she is doing when it comes to picking "investments." The world of investment is so vast and the opinions on what are the "right' or "best" ways to manage money are so diverse that it would be very difficult to cover that in a book. Additionally, I don't profess to be a money manager or have significant knowledge in that area; and, therefore, it would not be prudent for me to cover that in this book. In other words, you are on your own when trying to determine if your stock broker is picking the right stocks or mutual funds for you.

Finally, the following list is NOT an exhaustive list. A "good advisor" will know many of the following (if not all) and many more concepts/products to help clients accomplish their financial/estate/asset protection goals.

## Asset Protection

**Domestic Asset Protection**—Fraudulent Transfers; Retirement Plans; Typical Asset Protection Plans (that do not always work); Corporate Entities; Limited Liability Companies/Family Limited Partnerships; Trusts as Asset Protection Tools; Personal Residence Protection; Accounts Receivable (A/R) Asset Protection.

**Offshore Asset Protection**—Offshore Limited Liability Companies (LLCs); Offshore Trusts; Closely Held Insurance Companies (CICs).

## Basic Estate-Planning

Wills; Durable Powers of Attorney; A&B, Marital, or Living Trusts; Irrevocable Life Insurance Trusts (ILIT); Dynasty Trusts; Divorce Protection.

## Advanced Estate -Planning

Family Limited Partnerships; General Partnerships; Limited Partnerships; IRS Challenges; Discounting Strategies; Gifting Strategies; Freeze Partnerships; Preferred/Non-Preferred Interests; Grantor Retained Annuity Trusts; Generation-Skipping Tax-Planning Issues; Intentionally Defective Grantor Trusts; Structured Sales; Self-Canceling Installment Notes; Captive Insurance Companies.

## Charitable Planning

Split Interest Gifts; Charitable Gift Annuities; Charitable Remainder Trusts; Charitable Remainder Annuity Trusts; Charitable Remainder Unitrusts; Donor Advised Funds; Charitable Lead Trusts; Grantor Lead Trusts; Non-grantor Lead Trusts; Private Foundations.

## Life Insurance

**Types of Term Life Insurance Policies**—Guaranteed Level Term; Annually Renewable Term; Return of Premium Term; Conversion Privileges.

**Cash Value Life Insurance**—Cash Surrender Value; Cash Account Value; Policy Withdrawals; Modified Endowment Contracts; Policy Loans; Whole Life Insurance; Universal Life; Variable Universal Life; Equity Indexed Universal Life; Survivorship or "2nd-to-die" Life Insurance; Underwriting.

### Premium Finance Life Insurance

Theory Behind Premium Financing; Client Profile; Benefits of Premium Financing Using an ILIT; Types of Premium Financing Plans (Premium Financed and Premium and Interest Finances); The Economics of Premium Financing (Interest Rates, Policy Crediting Rates, Collateral Requirements, Additional Collateral, Recourse Loans); Exit Strategies; Gift Tax Considerations; Personal Guarantees; Non-recourse Loan Arrangements.

### Tax-Deferred Annuities

Withdrawals; Investment Protection; Payment Options; Death Benefits; Surrender Charges; Market Value Adjustment; Penalties; Borrowing from an Annuity; Bonus Premiums; Penalty Free Withdrawals; Spousal Option; Annuitization; Taxation; Sales Loads; Aggregation Rule; Variable Annuities; Fixed Annuities; Single Premium Immediate Annuity; Single Premium Deferred Annuity; Tax Shelter Annuities; Traditional Fixed Annuities; Linked Fixed Annuities; Crediting Methods; Participation Rate; Guaranteed Income Riders; Total Return Fixed Annuities; and Two-Tier Annuities.

### IRAs

Contribution Limits; Income Limits for Contributing; Deductibility Limits; Tax Credits; Roth IRAs; Roth IRA Conversion (good or bad); Rollovers; Transfers; Educational IRAs; Investment Limitations of IRAs; Investing in Real Estate, the Proper Use of Annuities; Prohibited Transaction Rules; Unrelated Business Income Taxes; Active Business Income; Debt Financed Income; Controlling IRA Assets from the Grave.

### Qualified Retirement Plans

Simplified Employee Pensions; Savings Incentive Match Plan for Employees IRA; Solo 401(k) Plans; 401(k) Plans; Roth 401(k) Plans; Top Heavy Concerns; Safe Harbor Rules; Money Purchase Plans; Profit Sharing Plans (Integrated, Age-Weighted, New Comparability); Nondiscrimination Testing; Defined Benefit Plans; Envelope Funding vs. Split Funding; "Carve-Out" Defined Benefit Plans; Cash Balance Plans; 412(e)(3) Defined Benefit Plans; Over-Funded Plans; Under-Funded Plans; Controlled Group Issues; Affiliated Service Group Issues; 401(h) Plans.

### The 70-80% Tax Trap

If you have assets in excess of the estate tax exemption amount AND money in a tax-deferred qualified plan or IRA, those assets could have a 70%-80% tax levied upon them at your death (the tax trap). Most advisors do not know this tax problem exists. Most who do have no idea how to solve it or mitigate it. A "good advisor" will know how to help you mitigate this tax problem through concepts such as Liquidate and Leverage or IRA/Pension Rescue.

### Employee Stock Ownership Plans (ESOPs)

Few advisors understand the power and usefulness of ESOPs as a viable planning tool. ESOPs allow business owners to sell their businesses to their employees and receive capital gains tax deferral on the sale of the stock. There are several different types of ESOP transactions that can be useful to either small closely held businesses or large Fortune 500 companies.

### Closely Held Insurance Companies (CICs)

CICs are one of if not the most powerful tax-favorable/wealth-building tools available to small business owners. Like ESOPs, few advisors know anything about them. The following is a list of some of the items an advisor should know about CICs: Single Parent Captives (Wholly-Owned); Group Captives; Entrepreneurial Captives; Domicile Selection; Partner Selection; Operating a Captive; Group or Association Captive; Rental Captives; Segregated Protected Cells; and the Affordable Captive Structure.

### Section 79 Plans

These are employee benefit plans used by business owners to buy individually owned cash value life insurance policies where the premium is 35%-45% deductible to the business. What's important to know about Section 79 Plans is that they are NOT economically viable and that there are many abuses in the industry when it comes to selling and setting these plans up properly. This topic is on my list of ones advisors should know not because it should be recommended to clients but because "good advisors" need to know what's wrong with them so they can counsel their clients not to use them.

### College-Planning—A Wealth Preservation Challenge

Financial Aid; Criteria for Financial Aid; Need Based Aid; Needs Analysis Formula; Cost of Attendance; Expected Family Contribution; Federal Methodology Formula and the FAFSA Forms; Institutional Methodology Formula and the CSS Profile Forms; Need vs. Aid; Non-Assessable Assets; Non-Assessable Income; Financial Aid Income and Benefits; Resources; Merit Based Aid; Private Scholarships: Student Loans; Tax Incentives (Federal); Hope Scholarship Credit; Lifetime Learning Credit; Student Loan Interest Deduction; Deduction for Qualified Higher Education Expenses; Penalty Free IRA Withdrawals; Tax Strategies; I-Bonds; Traditional IRA's; Roth IRA's; Tax Efficient Mutual Funds; Annuities; QTP's or 529 Plans; Coverdell Education Savings Accounts; College Planning Using Cash Value Life Insurance (CAUTION).

### Life Settlements

Why sell a life insurance policy; What type of life insurance policies can be sold; The Viator; Brokers; Tax Consequences; NAIC Disclosures; Estate-Planning Benefits; Health Expense Benefits; Term Conversion; Key-Man Policies; HIPPA.

### Mortgages/Equity Harvesting

Type of Loans—FHA; VA; RHS Loan Programs; State and Local Housing Programs; Conforming Loans; Jumbo Loans; B/C Loans; Fixed-Rate Mortgages; Balloon Loans; Adjustable Rate Mortgages; Margins; Negatively Amortizing Loans; Indexes

(Constant Maturity Treasury; Treasury Bill; 12-Month Treasury Average; 11th District Cost of Funds Index; London Inter Bank Offering Rates; Certificates of Deposit; Prime Rate); Equity Harvesting (also known as Equity Stripping).

### Medicaid Planning

Ethics of Medicaid Planning; Divestment Planning (Serial Divestment; Half-a-Loaf Planning; Reverse Half-a-Loaf Planning; Reverse Half-a-Loaf Planning with a Medicaid Compliant Annuity); Pre-"Look Back" Planning; Annuities and Trusts; Annuities that Qualify for Exclusion; Trusts that Qualify for Exclusion; Medicaid Annuity Trust; Supplemental Needs (d)(4)(A) Trusts and (d)(4)(C) Pooled Trusts; Immediate Need Medicaid Planning; Establishing Medicaid Eligibility; Major Asset Exclusions; Countable Resources; How to Categorize and Protect Resources; Medicaid Compliant Annuities; Medicaid Trusts; Income Qualification Rules; The Minimum Monthly Maintenance Need Allowance; How to Pay Nursing Home Costs during the Penalty Period; Divorce as an Option; Follow up (Post-Eligibility) Planning; Estate Recovery; Undue Hardship Waivers; Exempt Transfers.

### Long-Term Care Insurance

What Type of Coverage Should Clients Buy; How Do Clients Receive Benefits; Which Daily Benefit Should a Client Select; When and Why is Inflation Protection Appropriate; What Length of Coverage Should a Client Buy; What Elimination Period Should a Client Select; How Important is a Non-Forfeiture Option; 100% Tax Deductible LTC Premiums; Return of Premium LTC Insurance; State Incentives; Asset Based Long-Term Care; Qualified-LTCI Benefits.

### Disability Insurance

Disability vs. Death; Likelihood of Disability; Types of Disability Policies (Individual; Group; High-Risk; Special-Risk; Business Overhead Expense; Disability Buyout; Pension Protection Insurance); What to Look for in a Disability Policy (Renewability Provision; Guaranteed Renewable; Non-Cancelable and Guaranteed Renewable; Own Occupation; Modified Own Occupation; Any Occupation); Hybrid Definitions; Elimination

Period; Waiver of Premium; Capital Sum Benefit; Rehabilitation Benefit; Disability Insurance Exclusions and Limitations; Optional Riders (Residual Disability Rider; Cost Of Living Adjustment Rider; Future Increase Option Rider); Taxation of Benefits.

### Health Insurance

HIPAA/Kennedy-Kassabaum Bill; COBRA; Fully Insured Plans; Health Reimbursement Accounts; Partially Self-Funded Plans; Prescription Drug Card 'Carve-Out' Plans; Section 125 Plans; Health Savings Accounts.

### SUMMARY ON CONCEPTS/PRODUCTS "GOOD ADVISORS" SHOULD KNOW

If the previous list seems like a lot of information on a very diverse subject matter, that's because it is.

If you have any amount of wealth, I think you owe it to yourself to seek out an advisor who is familiar with most, if not all, of the items listed in this chapter.

Are there advisors out there who have a working knowledge of the concepts/products listed in this chapter? Absolutely. I've educated hundreds of advisors through The Wealth Preservation Institute on the topics covered in this chapter.

Does that mean that only advisors who have taken training know the topics covered in this chapter? Not necessarily; however, as you probably know or will find out when you try to find a "good advisor," most advisors do not want to provide clients with comprehensive advice. They want to work in a niche area and only provide advice on a narrow subject matter or work with a narrow band of products.

There is nothing wrong per se with working with a narrow group of concepts or products AS LONG AS that is disclosed to potential clients who can then choose to work with the advisor or seek out an advisor with a more well-rounded knowledge base (or one that works with a team of advisors to provide comprehensive advice)

The problem in the financial services and insurance industries is that there is very little disclosure about what advisors know and what they can sell or choose to sell. It is for this very reason that I decided to write this book to empower people with the needed knowledge so they could know how to identify a "good advisor" from a "bad advisor."

# **Chapter 11**
## **Real-World Horror Stories**

The title of the first chapter of this book is: "Everyone's Worst Nightmare."

In Chapter 1, I went over a few made-up horror stories that I pieced together from my discussions with advisors over the last few years.

The following are the example nightmare clients:

-80-year old widow with assets of less than $1 million

-Middle-class, 67 year old who retired in 2007

-65-year old multi-millionaire

-Middle-class, 45 year old

-30-year old who just got married

To say that this book is unique I think is an understatement. I've tried to put together a book that gives readers an insider's view of many different industries in a way that is somewhat scandalous.

The vast majority of those who read this book will look back at the advice given to them by various advisors and will be outraged.

The advice given on a daily basis by "bad advisors" is an outrage to me and is the reason I wrote this book.

The coup de gras for this book is the access readers will have to real-world horror stories.

### **WHAT IS A REAL-WORLD HORROR STORY?**

It's when a real person who is given bad advice tells his/her story.

It's a story an advisor tells after taking on a new client who has had advice given to him/her by a "bad advisor."

## POSTING AND READING REAL-WORLD HORROR STORIES

When I decided to write this book, I knew a significant portion of the book would actually not be in the book at all. It would be online at the website for the book, www.badadvisors.com.

On the book's website is a message board that advisor and non-advisor readers of this book can post real-world horror stories for others to read.

For example, an advisor might meet with a 75-year old client who lives on a fixed income from a pension plan and Social Security; and she has an additional $200,000 in CDs.

The client might have recently met with an insurance advisor who tried to sell her an annuity that has a 15-year surrender charge and little access to her money in the early years.

This could be a horror story because a 75-year old client typically should not be purchasing annuities with 15-year surrender charges (limiting access to money for a 15-year period for someone who has a life expectancy of less than 10 years doesn't make much financial sense).

The story could be changed a bit where the advisor, instead of putting the client into a 15-year surrender-charge annuity, told her to put all her liquid wealth into mutual funds. Again, this is not prudent advice for a client of her age and financial makeup (her money should not be at risk in the market).

### MONITORING THE MESSAGE BOARD

The message board will be monitored and censored so fake stories can't be posted. Also, no names of clients will be used on the blog or of anyone else who doesn't want to be identified.

Once a story has been approved for the message board, those who are signed up will be notified through e-mail that a new one has been posted. Additionally, the story will stay on the blog for months to come so those who sign up after a story has been posted can read older posts.

## HOW DO YOU SIGN UP FOR THE HORROR-STORY MESSAGE BOARD?

All you have to do to sign up for the blog is go to www.badadvisors.com and find on the front page of the site the sign-up link.

Once you sign up, you'll be sent a confirmation e-mail. Once you confirm that you want to sign up, you'll be able to post on the blog yourself or simply be able to read the posts of others.

# Help from the Author

My guess is that most people who read this entire book will have a laundry list of questions they'd like answers to as it pertains to advice various advisors have given them over the years.

The question I had for myself is: Where are readers going to find the answers to questions about their potentially "bad advisors"?

You don't want to go to the advisor you think is giving you bad advice.

You could go to another advisor in the same field and ask questions, but how do you know if that advisor is a "good" or "bad advisor"?

In order for readers to get the maximum benefit from this book, I knew I would have to create a forum or place where I could answer specific questions.

### "BAD ADVISORS" MESSAGE BOARD

If you go to www.badadvisors.com, you will be able to sign up for a message board. Once registered (and you can use a no-name username so no one knows who you are), you can **ask me any questions you'd like** about your potentially "bad advisor."

I will post a message that will be forwarded to you directly and will be posted on the message board. Your question will also stay on the board for others to read and learn from.

It is my hope that over time many of the classic is my advisor a "bad advisor" questions will be posted and answered; and after a period of time, a nice log of useful questions and answers will amass.

### GETTING ANSWERS BEFORE YOU ASK QUESTIONS

You may have heard the saying that when attorneys are cross examining a witness on the stand they should never ask a question that they don't know the answer to.

Why is that? Because they may get an answer they don't like or that will be harmful to the case.

The analogy isn't prefect when comparing it to asking questions of potentially "bad advisors," but you really do want to know most of the answers to the questions you'll be asking your potentially "bad advisors" before you ask them.

Why?

The main reason is that, if you already know the answer or what you think is the answer, when the advisor tries to give you a B.S. response, you'll know the advisor is full of it.

Being armed with knowledge before you talk with an advisor is definitely the way to get to the bottom of things and is the reason I wrote this book and created the www.badadvisors.com message board.

**URGENT SITUATION**

There will be people who read this book who will be so freaked out over what they've read and the advice they've been given that they will literally be on the verge of shaking because of fear or anger or both. Why? Because some readers will know that the advice they've been given has cost them tens if not hundreds of thousands of dollars.

If you have an urgent need to have questions answered about the bad advice you've been given and what you can do to mitigate or stop the damage, please feel free to e-mail me at roccy@badadvisors.com. I will typically be able to get back with you within 24 hours.

If it is something that is so time critical that you can't wait for an e-mail response, please feel free to call me at 269-216-9978. If I can't pick up, I'll do my best to get back with you ASAP.

**EDUCATIONAL INFORMATION**

One way you can get help or help yourself is by going to www.wealthpreservationinstitute.com. On the website, you can read more information on the topics covered in this book. There are also several voiced-over presentations you can view/listen to.

### FINDING "GOOD ADVISORS"

Invariably when people read my books, X amount of them will call me and ask me if I can personally take them on as clients.

It's rare for me to take on a new client these days. My primary business is to educate CPAs/EAs/accountants, attorneys, financial planners/CFPs, and insurance agents on how to provide the best client-first advice to their clients.

Because I've literally trained thousands of advisors over the years, I usually will have someone in a local area that a potential client can meet with.

Rest assured, advisors who I recommend are very familiar with what's in this book and my other books and know that their level of customer service that needs to be given to clients better be at the highest level. The advisors I've trained know that potential clients I refer out have the ability and are even encouraged to contact me if they think the advice given to them by an advisor I referred them to does not seem very good or is not giving advice that is in the client's best interest.

### How do you find an advisor in your local area?

Simply e-mail me at roccy@badadvisors.com with your request or go to www.badadvisors.com, and you'll be able to fill out a request form. Once my office receives that form, you will be contacted for a phone call with me so I can assess your situation and make sure I'm referring you to an advisor best suited to help fulfill your needs.

### DID AN ADVISOR GIVE YOU MY BOOK?

While you might think an advisor would be crazy to hand you my book, many advisors will do just that. Advisors will buy multiple copies of my book to hand to current clients and potential clients.

While I will not know every advisor personally who hands out my book, what I can state is that the advisor certainly has read the book and knows the standards he/she must live up to in order to not be considered a "bad advisor." This is a good sign, and it is likely that the advisor is one who is confident that his/her advice is beyond question and what I would consider client-first advice.

## BOOK REVIEW

If you are so motivated in a good or bad way from reading this book, I would appreciate your feedback. Positive feedback confirms that the way I write books is understandable and helpful to readers.

If you want to provide constructive criticism (or complain) about something in the book or the way I wrote something, please feel free to submit such comments. That will help me when I update the book (which I will do on an annual basis); and since it is my goal to put forth the best book I can, negative or constructive comments are welcome.

Thank you for reading this book, and I encourage you to educate yourself and think critically so you don't get taken advantage of by a "bad advisor."